GUID Color Backroads & 4-Wheel Drive Trails Vol. 2

By **CHARLES A. WELLS**

Easy • Moderate • Difficult
Backcountry Driving Adventures

FunTreks, Inc.

Published by FunTreks, Inc.
P.O. Box 49187, Colorado Springs, CO 80949-9187
Phone:(719) 536-0722   E Mail: funtreks@pcisys.net

Copyright © 1999 by FunTreks, Inc.

Edited by Sharon Krall

Cover design, photography, maps, and production by Charles A.Wells

First Edition

Library of Congress Catalog Card Number 98-93117
ISBN 0-9664976-1-9

Produced in the United States of America

HOW TO ORDER MORE BOOKS:

Use Order Blanks at back of book. If missing, see information below:
Telephone orders: Call Toll Free: 1(877) 222-7623. We accept VISA or
MasterCard. Please have your card ready when you call.
Mail Orders: Send check plus name, address, and telephone number to:
FunTreks, Inc. P.O. Box 49187, Colorado Springs, CO 80949-9187.
Cost: $15.95 per book plus $4.00 shipping for first book and $2.00 for each addi-
tional book. Add 3% tax for books shipped to Colorado.
Guarantee: Money back if not satisfied, no questions asked.

DISCLAIMER

Travel in the Colorado backcountry is by its very nature potentially
dangerous and could result in property damage, injury, or even death.
The scope of this book cannot predict every possible hazard you may
encounter. If you drive any of the trails in this book, you acknowledge
these risks and assume full responsibility. You are the final judge as to
whether a trail is safe to drive on any given day, whether your vehicle is
capable of the journey, and what supplies you should carry. The information contained herein cannot replace good judgment and proper
preparation on your part. The publisher and author of this book disclaim
any and all liability for bodily injury, death, or property damage that
could occur to you or any of your passengers.

ACKNOWLEDGMENTS

My explorations have taken me across endless miles of Colorado into unfamiliar backcountry. To facilitate my search for outstanding trails, I asked local residents and members of local four-wheel drive clubs for assistance. Their response was overwhelming. Complete strangers graciously set aside personal time to show me their favorite trails, read over my trail descriptions, and inspect my finished maps for accuracy. This local input has added depth and insight to the book. I am indebted to each of these friendly people for their assistance. Although it is impossible to mention everyone I met along the way, I would like to give special recognition to the following persons and organizations:

The Larimer County Four-Wheelers Club in Fort Collins. Thanks to all of you who participated in club runs set up specifically for my benefit. A special thanks to Craig Stumbough, president of the club who organized and led most of the runs and helped proof final pages. In addition, as a key member of the state four-wheel drive association and *1998 Colorado Four-Wheeler of the Year*, Craig put me in touch with many helpful people across the state.

The Grand Mesa Four-Wheelers Club in Grand Junction. I especially thank Roy Joseph, president. Roy invited me on a club run then spent several days giving me a personal tour of the Grand Junction area. I stayed overnight at his home as we pored over maps late into the night.

Lydia Constantini, manager of the Columbine Cabins north of Steamboat Springs. Lydia, a resident of historic Columbine, directed me to some trails in Area 4, then helped proof final pages.

Gail Straty, Phil Johnsey, and Lisa Johnsey of the Trailridge Runners Four-Wheel Drive Club in Longmont. They answered questions about trails in Areas 2 and 3 and helped proof final pages.

My own club, the Colorado Four-Wheelers, in Colorado Springs. Active members Larry Leaveck, Neale Geis, Bob Niehoff, and Larry Miller are largely responsible for my four-wheeling interest and education.

Sharon Krall, for her careful and expeditious editing of this book.

Linda Meyer and Jim Magill, both experts in Macintosh graphics and digital prepress, continue to offer help and guidance.

My immediate family and wife, Beverly, who encouraged me to continue in what has now become a full-time job.

And finally, the U.S. Forest Service, the Bureau of Land Management, Tread Lightly!,® and the BlueRibbon Coalition, who, in addition to trail advice, helped teach me the importance of responsible land use and how we must all work together to preserve our ever-threatened backcountry.

Tread Lightly! is a registered trademark of Tread Lightly!, Inc.

Jamestown/ Ward Road, Trail #14, rated moderate.

Contents

Trails Listed by Area

65 more trails can be found in the author's original guidebook

GUIDE TO
Colorado Backroads & 4-Wheel Drive Trails

EASY Family Fun Runs

MODERATE Sport Utility Adventures

DIFFICULT Hard-Core Challenges

By Charles A. Wells

(See Page 171 for details)

Statewide Locator Map

Colorado

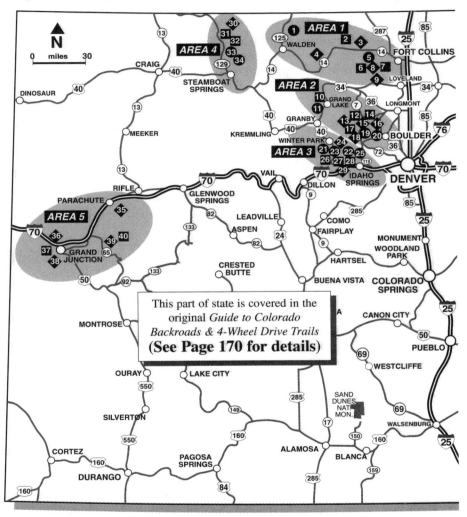

This part of state is covered in the original *Guide to Colorado Backroads & 4-Wheel Drive Trails*
(See Page 170 for details)

● Easy Trails
■ Moderate Trails
◆ Difficult Trails

See individual area maps for more detail.

Trails Listed by Difficulty

**Note: These trails have a substantial amount of easy and moderate terrain suitable for stock sport utility vehicles. Difficult sections of the trail are avoidable. Read individual trail descriptions.

Trail Ratings Defined

Trail ratings are very subjective. Descriptions attempt to describe worst case scenarios under good weather conditions, but not all situations are predictable. You must weigh your experience and confidence against the conditions of the day. Obviously not all of these conditions exist on every trail. Read each trail description carefully. The rating is based on the worst part of the trail. Remember, snow, ice, heavy rain, spring run-off, or other adverse conditions can increase the difficulty of a trail.

Easy

Graded dirt road with possible short stretches of rocks, ruts, and washed out areas. Gentle grades. Water depths could reach mid hubcap. Be more careful about water depths during heavy run-off periods. Full single lane or wider with adequate room to pass most of the time. Off-camber areas minimal. Four-wheel drive recommended on most trails but some are suitable for two-wheel drive under dry conditions. Read the description carefully to be sure.

Moderate

Rutted dirt or rocky road suitable for most sport utility vehicles. Four-wheel drive, low range, and high ground clearance required. Standard factory skid plates and tow hooks recommended on many trails. Rocks or holes may cause undercarriage to bottom out occasionally. Some grades fairly steep but manageable if dry. Some off-camber areas will require caution. Minimal narrow shelf roads. Water depths could reach bumper in a few situations. Be more careful about water depths during heavy run-off periods. Backing may be necessary to pass. Mud holes may be present.

Difficult

Generally suitable for more aggressive stock vehicles or modified vehicles. Lifts, differential lockers, aggressive articulation, and/or winches recommended on some trails. Skid plates and tow hooks required. Body damage possible on obstacles. Grades can be steep with severe ground undulation. Off-camber areas can be extreme. Water depths extremely deep. Shelf roads extremely narrow; full-size vehicles use caution and read trail description carefully. Passing may be difficult with backing required for long distances. Brush may scrape sides of vehicle. Deep mud bogs possible.

Trails Listed Alphabetically

AUTHOR'S FAVORITE TRAILS
SHOWN IN BOLD FACE TYPE

INTRODUCTION

Jenny Creek Road, Trail #24, rated difficult. This photo is not the difficult portion.

Introduction

When I published the original *Guide to Colorado Backroads and 4-Wheel Drive Trails* less than a year ago, my expectations were modest. Not in my wildest dreams could I have predicted the results. From day one, this book has been flying off shelves all over Colorado and surrounding states. Thousands of people have bought and enjoyed the book. I've gotten calls and letters from happy customers from all over the world who tell me it is the best backroad guide they have ever used. Their next question is invariably—do you have any other books? Well now I can say "yes"—*Guide to Colorado Backroads & 4-Wheel Drive Trails Vol. 2*. Okay, so it's not the most creative title. But, at least it makes it clear what to expect—a guide equal to the original in quality and presentation.

Volume 2 contains 40 new trails close to major metropolitan areas of Colorado. Twenty-nine trails are close to Denver, Boulder, and Fort Collins; five are near Steamboat Springs; and six encircle Grand Junction. Whether you're a new SUV owner or a seasoned offroad veteran, you'll find plenty to enjoy. This book contains 11 easy trails, 14 moderate trails, and 15 difficult trails. Three of the difficult trails have significant expanses of easy and moderate terrain making a total of 28 trails suitable for most stock sport utility vehicles. All trails have clear instructions, abundant photographs, and easy-to-follow maps.

Where space permits, I've included some history about each trail. My historical sketches, however, because of limited space, provide only a paltry taste of what's available. To enhance your backcountry experience, I encourage you to look through the references at the end of this book and read as much as possible. In particular, I recommend the outstanding books of Robert L. Brown, who has devoted his life to the history of Colorado Ghost Towns. Many of the trails in this book exist because of these forgotten towns, most now completely gone.

HOW TO USE THIS BOOK

This book has been designed for quick and easy use. Trails are grouped by area. First use the state locator map on page 7 to determine the big picture, then turn to each area map for more detail. Each trail is shown with photos and a map. All maps are to scale and oriented with north at the top. Scale is indicated using an overall grid. Check the size of the grid at the bottom of each map. A small legend or "Mini Key" is included on each map for quick reference. Find the full map legend on page 30.

The shaded portion of the trail is described in the text. Other roads are for reference only and should be traveled at your own risk. Water crossing and bridge symbols show major stream locations. Read each map for boundary designations. Trails are described in one direction with the starting point clearly indicated. In certain cases, additional directions are given to the other end of the trail.

Trails are listed three ways for your convenience: by area on page 6, by difficulty on page 8, and alphabetically on page 10. Geometric shapes are used to indicate difficulty. A circle indicates easy, a square moderate, and a diamond difficult. Trail ratings are described in detail on page 9. Finer difficulty ratings can be determined by the order of the trails on page 8. Each trail listed is progressively more difficult than the last, although distinctions from one trail to the next may be negligible.

The text for each trail includes: general location, difficulty details, special features, approximate length and driving time, details of the drive, directions home, location of nearest services, and other maps. Other activities and historical highlights are shown for some trails.

Mileages can vary because of vehicle differences and driving habits. Readings were rounded to the nearest tenth of a mile.

The appendix of this book includes a glossary, a list of references and recommended reading, helpful addresses and phone numbers, and an index.

SELECTING THE RIGHT TRAIL FOR YOUR VEHICLE

Today's modern sport utility vehicles are amazingly well designed for off-highway travel. Modern technology is making the backcountry accessible to ever more capable stock vehicles. More and more people are buying sport utilities and setting out to discover the fun that other SUV owners are having. Sometimes, however, beginners think that once they buy a four-wheel drive vehicle, it will go anywhere. They soon learn that this is not the case. The following will help you decide which trails are right for your vehicle.

Easy: Suitable for all stock four-wheel drive sport utility vehicles with high ground clearance and low range. Some trails can be driven in two-wheel drive without low range in dry weather. A few trails, under ideal conditions, are suitable for passenger cars.

Moderate: Suitable for most stock sport utility vehicles with high ground clearance and low range. For the toughest moderate trails, factory skid plates, tow hooks, and all-terrain tires are recommended. These options are available from your dealer or local four-wheel drive shop.

Difficult: Suitable for some stock sport utility vehicles with very high ground clearance, excellent articulation, tow hooks, and a full skid plate package. All-terrain tires as a minimum, mud terrains preferred. A winch or differential lockers are recommended for the most difficult trails. Drivers who spend a great deal of time on extreme trails find it advantageous to modify their vehicles with higher ground clearance, oversized tires, and heavy duty accessories.

(These are general descriptions. Read each trail description carefully for more detail.)

IMPORTANT FACTS ABOUT COLORADO

Although similar to other Rocky Mountain states, Colorado is unique in many ways. If you are new to mountain driving, read this part carefully.

It's a big place. Colorado is a large state by eastern standards. When I first moved here from Ohio almost 20 years ago, I was surprised at how long it took to get from one place to another. When traveling to trails, check the scale of the map and determine the total number of miles to your destination. Then allow plenty of time to get there. Terrain varies considerably from one part of the state to the other, so the landscape will likely be quite different at your destination. Allow extra time for slower speeds on winding roads and washboard roads. Fortunately, the drive to the trail can be as beautiful as the trail itself. So take your time, be patient, and enjoy the ride.

When to go. The length of the four-wheel drive season in Colorado depends on the elevation of the trail. A few trails at low elevations open in late April or early May. More trails open in late May and June. High mountain passes typically are passable the first or second week in July but a winter of heavy snows may mean even later. The best time of year to find most trails open is in August and September. (Check with the U.S. Forest Service to be sure. See Appendix for phone numbers.) September also is the peak time to enjoy the changing colors of the aspens. You may squeeze in some very late season wheeling in early October if no early winter snow has fallen. But be aware the regular Colorado hunting season begins the second week of October.

Start as early as possible in the day. Mornings are usually clear while afternoons are often cloudy with a greater chance of thunderstorms. Allow a sizable margin of daylight for your return trip to avoid being on the trail at night.

The weather. Colorado weather is often very pleasant and more moderate than people expect. Low humidity at high elevations keeps temperatures cool in the summer. In the winter, the sun shines most of the time and it stays relatively warm. There are few flies and mosquitoes except around wetlands. Trails in the Grand Junction area get a little buggy during the hot summer months. The downside to Colorado weather is that it is very unpredictable and can be extreme at times. Although it doesn't happen frequently, it can snow anytime during the summer, especially at higher elevations and at night when temperatures drop. Colorado can also be very windy. Pack

14

plenty of warm clothing regardless of how hot it might be when you depart. Also, make sure you drink plenty of fluids to help you adapt to the dry thin air. Use sunscreen because you will sunburn quicker.

Changing road conditions. Colorado loves to surprise you. Watch for unexpected ice, snow, landslides, avalanches, fallen trees, washouts, deep water, and leaping deer. A clay surface road can be passable when dry but very slippery if wet.

Lightning. Thunderstorms, hail, and lightning are very common in Colorado, especially in the late afternoon. Stay below timberline if you see a storm approaching. If you get stuck above timberline, a hardtop vehicle offers more safety from lightning than being outside, but don't touch anything metal inside your vehicle. Lightning can strike from a distant storm even when it is sunny overhead.

Fires and floods. Although extremely rare, you must be aware of the possibility of forest fires and flash floods. Fires can move quickly, so watch for smoke when you are at higher points. At certain times of year, fire danger can be extremely high and the Forest Service will post fire danger warnings. During these times, campfires may be prohibited. Fines can be very steep for violators. Heavy rainstorms can cause flash floods at any time during the spring and summer. The danger is particularly acute if you are in a narrow canyon (like the Big Thompson Canyon described in Storm Mountain Trail #9). If you have reason to believe a flash flood is imminent, do not try to outrun it in your car. Abandon your car and climb to higher ground. Most flash flood deaths occur in vehicles.

Altitude sickness. Some people experience nausea, dizziness, headaches, or weakness the first time at high altitude. This condition usually improves over time. To minimize symptoms, give yourself time to acclimate, drink plenty of fluids, decrease salt intake, reduce alcohol and caffeine, eat foods high in carbohydrates, and try not to exert yourself. If symptoms become severe, the only sure remedy is to return to a lower altitude. Consult your doctor before going to higher altitudes if you have health problems.

Hypothermia. Hypothermia is possible even in the summer. If you get caught in a sudden shower at high altitude, your body temperature can drop suddenly. Always take rain gear and extra clothing.

Don't drink the water. No matter how cool, clear, or refreshing a mountain stream or lake may appear, never drink the water. Don't let anyone convince you that high altitude water is safe. If you must drink mountain water, boil it or use iodine tablets for purification. These are available at most sporting goods stores in Colorado. Carry your own drinking water.

Mine shafts, tunnels, and old structures. Be careful around old mine buildings. Do not enter or climb on any structures. Stay away from mine shafts and tunnels. Do not let children play in these areas.

RULES OF THE ROAD
The laws of Colorado.
• Most trails require that you be licensed, street legal, and carry a valid driver's license if driving.

• Vehicles traveling uphill always have the right of way, but use common sense. If you are closer to a wide spot, move over for the other vehicle.

• Don't drink and drive.

• All vehicles including mountain bikes are prohibited in Wilderness areas.

Forest Service rules.
• Travel only on roads with signs displaying a Forest Service number, or in some forests, a small white arrow.

• Stay on the trail at all times. Don't take shortcuts at switchbacks, or drive around bad spots. Sometimes other drivers take shortcuts that you know are not responsible. Don't use their tracks as an excuse to make the same mistake. This is how illegal trails get started.

• Trails are closed for valid reasons that may not be apparent to you. Do not under any circumstances enter a closed trail.

• Forest Service roads frequently pass through private property. If a gate is unlocked, and there are no "no trespassing" signs on the gate, it is usually okay to pass through, but make sure you leave the gate the way you found it. Close gate if indicated. When following a Forest Service road across private property, stay on the trail at all times.

• Pack out your trash except in fee areas that have approved receptacles. Never throw your trash into pit toilets.

• Never drive across open meadows. Do not walk or drive on delicate tundra, pick wildflowers, or remove anything from mining or other historical sights.

• Camp within 300 feet of the road.

• Don't park your vehicle in tall grass. The intense heat from your catalytic converter may start a fire.

• Human waste should be buried 6 to 8 inches deep at least 200 feet from any water source, campsite, or trail. Keep a small shovel handy for this purpose. If possible carry a portable camping toilet.

• Consult Forest Service maps for special land use regulations.

Trail Etiquette.
• Drive slowly and use caution at all times, especially around blind curves.

• Try to be as quiet as possible. Don't play your radio loudly, gun your engine, or spin your tires. Use your horn sparingly for emergencies only. Smile and be courteous to everyone. Help create a positive image for four-wheeling.

• Always pull over to the side of the road when you are out of your vehicle or not moving. Pull over for bikers and hikers. Stop and shut off your engine for horses and pack animals.

• Avoid crossing streams if possible, but if you must cross, do it at designated crossings only.

    • If someone overtakes you, pull over and let them pass.

    • Control your pets at all times. Don't let them bark or chase wildlife.

Camping guidelines.

• Use developed or existing campsites whenever possible.

• Camp away from streams, lakes, hiking trails, and historical mining sites. Leave as much distance as possible between you and other campers. Respect the privacy of others.

• Use a gas stove if possible and try to avoid fires. If you must have a fire, build it inside a fire ring of rocks, preferably one that is already there. Bring your own firewood if possible. Don't cut trees or branches. Let the fire burn itself out so only ashes remain. Spread the ashes to make sure they are cold. If you must douse the fire, do it thoroughly. If you've thrown bottles or cans into the fire that have not disintegrated, pack them as trash.

• Avoid using soap if at all possible and never around lakes or streams. Heat water to clean utensils. If you must use soap to bathe, use as little as possible. Do not bathe in or near a lake or stream.

• Plan your trip carefully and prepack your food in plastic bags or reusable containers. There will be less trash to haul away.

• Inspect the area thoroughly before leaving and make sure nothing is left lying around. The goal is to leave the area the way you found it or better.

SAFETY TIPS

Wear your seat belt. You might think that because you are driving slowly, it's not necessary to wear your seat belt or use child restraints. I've learned through experience that you are much safer with a seatbelt than without. Buckle up at all times.

Keep heads, arms, and legs inside moving vehicle. Many trails are narrow. Brush, tree limbs, and rock overhangs may come very close to your vehicle. The driver must make it clear to every passenger to stay inside the vehicle at all times. Children, in particular, must not be allowed to stick their heads, arms, or legs out the windows.

Extra maps. The maps in this book will clearly direct you along the trail. However, if you get lost or decide to venture down a spur road, you'll need additional maps with more detail. At the end of each trail description, I have listed other helpful maps. I recommend you get at least one of these maps. *National Forest Service maps* are the most commonly used. A scale of 1/2 inch to a mile is adequate. More than one map may be necessary if the trail crosses forest boundaries. Forest Service maps are usually the least expensive but are not frequently updated. More expensive but worth the money are *Trails Illustrated Topo Maps*. These maps are updated every year (stores may not have latest editions) and are made of durable waterproof plastic material. They include topographic information and the graphics are outstanding. Their only shortcoming is that they don't cover the entire state; however, they do cover most of the popular areas. Another map I strongly recommend is the *DeLorme Colorado Atlas & Gazetteer*. This is an over-sized atlas that breaks down the entire state into sections. If you look hard enough you can find almost every trail in this book. It has a lot of detail with some topographic information but the type is small. It is a handy size because you don't have to unfold it. Although it costs as much as several of the other maps, it's an excellent investment because of its statewide cover-age. All of these maps can be purchased at most larger bookstores and map stores. You can also buy Forest Service maps from your local National Forest Service office. Make sure you are buying the latest version available.

Spend a little time looking over the maps before you head out. Familiarize yourself as much as possible with the map and the area. When you get on the trail, don't be surprised to find inaccuracies on any of the maps. You can't always count on trail markers or road signs matching what is on the map. Sometimes signs have been updated but the maps have not. Many signs have been removed or vandalized.

Travel with another vehicle. Travel with other vehicles whenever pos-sible. If you must go alone, stay on the easier, more traveled routes. Never travel alone on difficult trails. Make sure you tell someone where you are going and your return time. Leave a plan of your route if possible. Report in at preset times or after you return.

If you can't find anyone to travel with you, call ahead or write to a four-wheel drive club in the specific area of your trip and ask for help. Make sure you explain your level of experience. To locate the club nearest you, call or write the Colorado Association of 4 Wheel Drive Clubs, Inc. (See address and phone number in back of book.)

Join a four-wheel drive club. Most clubs have runs on easy as well as difficult routes but ask to make sure. Select a club most appropriate for you.

If you get lost or stuck, stay with your vehicle unless you are very close to help. Your vehicle will provide shelter and is easier to see.

Inspect your vehicle carefully. Before you start into the backcountry, make sure your vehicle is in top operating condition. If you have a mechan-ic do the work, make sure he is reliable and understands four-wheeling. Tell him where you plan to take your vehicle. Pay particular attention to fluids, hoses, belts, battery, brakes, steering linkage, suspension system, driveline, and anything exposed under the vehicle. Tighten anything that may be loose. Inspect your tires carefully for potential weak spots and tread wear.

Supplies and equipment to take. No single list can be all inclusive. You must be the final judge of what you need. Here's a list of basic items:

❑ Plenty of food and water. Allow enough water for drinking and extra for the vehicle. Carry water purification tablets for emergencies.

❑ Extra clothing, shoes, socks, coats, and hats even in the summer. It gets very cold at night at higher elevations.

❑ Sleeping bags in case you get stuck overnight even if you are not planning to camp.

❑ A good first aid kit including sunscreen and insect repellent.

❑ Candle, matches, and a lighter.

❑ An extra set of keys and glasses.

❑ Toilet paper, paper towels, wet wipes, and trash bags.

❑ A large plastic sheet or tarp.

❑ Rain gear.

❑ Detailed maps, compass, watch, and a knife.

❑ If you plan to make a fire, carry your own firewood.

❑ Work gloves.

❑ A heavy duty tow strap.

❑ A fire extinguisher. Make sure you know where it is and can get to it easily.

❑ Jumper cables.

❑ Replacement fuses and electrical tape.

❑ Flashlight and extra batteries.

❑ A full tank of gas. If you carry extra gas make sure it is in an approved container and properly stored.

❑ A good set of tools.

❑ Baling wire and duct tape.

❑ An assortment of hose clamps, nuts, bolts, and washers.

❑ A full-size spare tire. Small emergency tires are not adequate in the backcountry.

❑ A tire pressure gauge, electric tire pump that will plug into your cigarette lighter, and a can of nonflammable tire sealant.

❑ A jack that will lift your vehicle fairly high off the ground. Take a small board to place under the jack. Carry a high lift jack if you can, especially on more difficult trails. Test your jack before you leave home.

❑ Shovel and axe. Folding shovels work great.

❑ Tire chains.

❑ CB radio and/or cellular phone.

❑ Portable toilet.

❑ If you have a winch, carry a tree strap, clevis, and snatch block.

Store these items in tote bags or large plastic containers so they can be easily loaded into your vehicle when it's time to go. Make sure you tie everything down thoroughly so it doesn't bounce around or shift.

Maintenance. Backroad travel puts your vehicle under greater stress than normal highway driving. Follow maintenance directions in your owners manual for severe driving conditions. This usually calls for changing your oil, oil filter, and air filter more frequently as well as more frequent fluid checks and lubrications. Inspect your tires carefully; they take a lot of extra abuse. After your trip, make sure you wash your vehicle. Use a high pressure spray to thoroughly clean the underside and wheel wells. Automatic car washes usually are not adequate. Do it yourself, if you want your vehicle in good shape for the next trip.

YOUR RESPONSIBILITIES AS A BACKCOUNTRY DRIVER

It is imperative that we educate ourselves on minimum impact driving techniques and diligently practice what we learn. If we don't, we will eventually lose our rights to use our remote lands. Fortunately, there are organizations whose goal is to educate the public on low impact recreational techniques. Two of the largest and most respected organizations are *Tread Lightly!, Inc.* and the *BlueRibbon Coalition.*

Tread Lightly!,® Inc. This national non-profit organization was established in 1990 to protect public and private lands by educating as many people as possible in the proper use of off-highway vehicles. It is supported by donations from corporate members including manufacturers of off-highway vehicles, environmental groups, user associations including many four-wheel drive clubs, government agencies, and people like you and me who are fighting to keep the backcountry open to enjoy. The suggestions of *Tread Lightly* are simple. Please read them, abide by them and pass them along to others.

- **T**ravel only where permitted
- **R**espect the rights of others
- **E**ducate yourself
- **A**void streams, meadows, wildlife areas, etc.
- **D**rive and travel responsibly

Join today. You'll receive many educational materials and be supporting a great cause. Your membership also includes a *Tread Lightly* bumper sticker, patch, lapel pin, quarterly newsletter, and other materials. Call or write to the address shown in appendix.

BlueRibbon Coalition. No group fights harder to keep public lands open for responsible vehicular use. Their motto is "Preserving Our Natural Resources *For* the Public Instead of *From* the Public." This organization has people in Washington constantly watching over your rights. They frequently testify at hearings on land use issues and constantly work to convince your congressmen of the importance of keeping the backcountry open. They publish the informative monthly *BlueRibbon Magazine,* which is full of interesting articles on the latest governmental actions affecting land use. It also includes educational articles and reports of fun vehicular activities that are happening all over the country. Join today. See appendix for address and phone number.

Four-wheel drive organizations. Other information specific to four-wheeling is available from the Colorado Association of 4 Wheel Drive Clubs, Inc. and the national United Four Wheel Drive Associations, Inc. Both of these organizations publish informative monthly newsletters. See appendix for addresses and phone numbers. If you are from outside Colorado, you probably have your own state four-wheel drive organization. Contact the United Four Wheel Drive Associations, Inc. for information.

BACKCOUNTRY DRIVING TECHNIQUES

The basics. It may surprise you to learn that many SUV owners have never shifted their vehicles into low range. I once encountered an SUV on the most dangerous part of Schofield Pass (described in the original guide). There were four vehicles in our group going uphill. Since he was a single vehicle and we had the right of way, we assumed he would back up and let us by. When he didn't, we asked him why. When he said he didn't have enough power to back up, we looked inside and noticed that he was not in low gear. When we pointed this out he seemed a little embarrassed. Apparently it never occurred to him what that other lever was for. It is situations like this that have provided extra motivation for me to write my first two guide books. I'd like to prevent others from getting themselves in such dangerous and helpless situations. If you read this book carefully, a similar situation is unlikely to happen to you. You'll recognize dangerous trails for which you are not yet ready, and when you are ready, you will know how to drive them safely.

If you have never shifted into low, grab your owner's manual now and start practicing. Read the rest of this book, then try some of the easy trails. Gradually you'll become more proficient and eventually you'll be ready to move up in difficulty.

Low and slow. Your vehicle was designed to go over rocky and bumpy terrain but only at slow speed. Get used to driving slowly in first gear low range. This will allow you to idle over obstacles without stalling. You don't need to shift back and forth constantly. Get into a low gear and stay there as much as possible so your engine can operate at high RPM and at maximum power. If you have a standard transmission, your goal should be to use your clutch as little as possible. As you encounter resistance on an obstacle or an uphill grade, just give it a little gas. As you start downhill, allow the engine's resistance to act as a brake. If the engine alone will not stop you from accelerating, then help a little with the brake. When you need more power but not more speed, press on the gas and feather the brake a little at the same time. This takes a little practice, but you will be amazed at the control you have. This technique works equally well with automatic transmissions.

Going clutchless. Standard transmissions can be safely started in first gear low range without depressing the clutch. The starter motor has the power, when geared down, to start the engine and car moving at the same time even on a steep hill. If you stall on a steep hill, simply turn the key to get moving again. This saves tremendous wear on the clutch. You'll look like a pro as your vehicle moves smoothly forward without jerking or rolling backwards. When it's time to stop the vehicle, simply turn off the key without depressing the clutch. Try it a few times and you'll see how easily it works. I repeat, you must be in first gear **low**. This technique will not work if you are totally jammed against a major obstacle or if your vehicle has a safety device that stops you from starting in gear.

Rocks and other high points. Never attempt to straddle a rock that is large enough to strike your differentials, transfer case or other low-hanging parts of your undercarriage. Instead, drive over the highest point with your tire, which is designed to take the abuse. This will lift your undercarriage over the obstacle. As you enter a rocky area, look ahead to determine where the high points are, then make every effort to cross them with your tires. Learn the low points of your undercarriage.

Using a spotter. Sometimes there are so many rocks you get confused about which way to go. In this case, have someone get out and guide you. They should stand at a safe distance in front, watching your tires and undercarriage. With hand signals, they can direct you left or right. If you are alone, don't be embarrassed to spot for yourself by getting in and out of your vehicle several times.

Those clunking sounds. Having made every attempt to avoid dragging bottom, you'll find it's not always possible. It is inevitable that a rock will contact your undercarriage eventually. The sound can be quite unnerving the first time it happens. If you are driving slowly and have proper skid plates, damage is unlikely. Look for a different line, back up and try again. If unsuccessful, see "Crossing large rocks" below.

Crossing a log. If the log is higher than your ground clearance, you will likely become high centered. Sometimes crossing at an angle helps. If you can't make it, build a ramp by stacking rocks on each side of the log. When done, put the rocks back where you found them. It might be possible to avoid driving over the log altogether by simply pulling the log to the side of the road with a tow strap or winch.

Crossing large rocks. Sometimes a rock is too large to drive over or at such a steep angle your bumper hits the rock before your tire. The solution is the same as crossing a log. Stack rocks on each side to form a ramp. Once over the obstacle, make sure you put the rocks back where you found them. The next driver to come along may prefer the challenge of crossing the rock in its more difficult state.

Getting high centered. You may drive over a large rock or into a rut, causing you to get lodged on the object. If this happens, don't panic. First ask your passengers to get out to see if less weight helps. Try rocking the vehicle. If this doesn't work, jack up your vehicle and place a few rocks under the tires so that when you let the jack down, you take the weight off the high point. Determine whether driving forward or reverse is best and try again. You may have to repeat this procedure several times if you are seriously high centered. Eventually you will learn what you can and cannot drive over.

Look in all directions. Unlike highway driving in which your primary need for attention is straight ahead, backcountry driving requires you to look in all directions. Objects can block your path from above, below, and from the sides. Trees fall, branches droop, and rocks slide, making the trail into an ever-changing obstacle course.

Scout ahead. If you are on an unfamiliar trail and are concerned that the trail is becoming too difficult, get out of your vehicle and walk the trail ahead of you. This gives you an opportunity to pick an easy place to turn around before you get into trouble. If you have to turn around, back up or pull ahead until you find a wide flat spot. Don't try to turn in a narrow confined area. This can damage the trail and perhaps tip over your vehicle.

Anticipate. Shift into four-wheel drive or low range before it is needed. If you wait until it is needed, conditions might be too difficult, e.g., halfway up a hillside.

Blind curves. When approaching blind curves, always assume that there is a speeding vehicle coming from the opposite direction. This will prepare you for the worst. Be aware that many people drive on the wrong side of the road to stay away from the outer edge of a trail. Whenever possible, keep your windows open and your radio off so that you can hear an approaching vehicle. You can usually hear motorcycles and ATVs. Quiet SUVs are the biggest problem. Collisions do occur so be careful.

Driving uphill. Use extreme caution when attempting to climb a hill. The difficulty of hill climbing is often misjudged by the novice four-wheeler. You should have good tires, adequate power, and be shifted into four-wheel drive low. There are four factors that determine difficulty:

Length of the hill. If the hill is very long, it is less likely that momentum will carry you to the top. Short hills are easier.

Traction. A rock surface is easier to climb than dirt.

Bumpiness. If the road surface undulates to the point where all four tires do not stay on the ground at the same time, you will have great difficulty climbing even a moderately steep hill.

Steepness. This can be difficult to judge, so examine a hill carefully before you attempt it. Walk up the hill if necessary to make sure it is not steeper at the top. If you are not absolutely sure you can climb a hill, don't attempt it. Practice on smaller hills first.

If you attempt a hill, approach it straight on and stay that way all the way to the top. Do not turn sideways or try to drive across the hill. Do not use excessive speed but keep moving at a steady pace. Make sure no one is coming up from the other side. Position a spotter at the top of the hill if necessary. Do not spin your tires because this can turn you sideways to the hill. If you feel you are coming to a stop due to lack of traction, turn your steering wheel back and forth quickly. This will give you additional grip. If you stall, use your brake and restart your engine. You may also have to use your emergency brake. If you start to slide backwards even with your brake on, you may have to ease up on the brake enough to regain steering control. Don't allow your wheels to lock up. If you don't make it to the top of the hill, shift into reverse and back down slowly in a straight line. Try the hill again but only if you think you learned enough to make a difference. As you approach the top of the hill, ease off the gas so you are in control before starting down the other side.

Driving downhill. Make sure you are in four-wheel drive. Examine the hill carefully and determine the best route that will allow you to go straight down the hill. Do not turn sideways. Use the lowest gears possible, allowing the engine's compression to hold you back. Do not ride the clutch. Feather the brakes slightly if additional slowing is needed. Do not allow the wheels to lock up. This will cause loss of steering and possibly cause you to slide sideways. The natural reaction when you begin to slide is to press harder on the brakes. Try to stay off the brakes. If you continue to slide despite these efforts, turn in the direction of the slide as you would on ice or snow and accelerate slightly. This will help maintain steering control.

Parking on a steep hill. Put your vehicle in reverse gear if pointing downhill and in forward gear if pointing uphill. For automatic transmissions, shift to park. Set your emergency brake hard. For extra insurance, block your tires.

Driving side hills. Side hill situations are dangerous so try to avoid them if possible. In Colorado, this will be difficult because off-camber situations are a fact of life. No one can tell you how far your vehicle can safely lean. You must learn the limitations through practice. Remember that sport utility vehicles have a higher center of gravity and are less stable than a passenger car. However, don't get paranoid. Your vehicle will likely lean a lot more than you think. Drive slowly to avoid bouncing over. A good way to learn is to watch an experienced driver with a vehicle similar to yours. This is an advantage to traveling with a group. Once you see how far other vehicles can lean, you will become more comfortable in these situations. Use extreme caution if the road surface is slippery from loose gravel, mud, or wet clay. Turn around if necessary.

Crossing streams and water holes. You must know the high water point of your vehicle before entering any body of water. Several factors can determine this point, including the height of the air intake and the location of the computer module (newer vehicles). Water sucked into the air intake is a very serious matter. If you don't know where these items are located, check with your dealer or a good four-wheel drive shop. A low fan can throw water on the engine and cause it to stall. You may have to disconnect your fan belt. Water can be sucked into your differentials so check them regularly after crossing deep streams.

After you understand your vehicle's capabilities, you must assess the stream conditions. First determine the depth of the water. If you are with a group, let the most experienced driver cross first. Follow his line if he is successful. If you are alone, you might wait for someone else to come along. Sometimes you can use a long stick to check the depth of small streams or water holes. Check for deep holes, large obstacles, and muddy sections. If you can't determine the water depth, don't cross. A winch line or long tow strap can be used as a safety line to pull someone back if he gets into trouble, but it must be attached before entering the water. It must also be long enough for him to reach shallow water on the other side. Once in the water, drive slowly but steadily. This creates a small wake which helps form an air pocket around the engine. I've seen people put a piece of cardboard or canvas over the front of their vehicle to enhance the wake affect. This only works if you keep moving. After exiting a stream, test your brakes. You may have to ride them lightly for a short distance until they dry out.

Always cross streams at designated water crossings. Don't drive in the direction of the stream. Try to minimize disruption of the water habitat.

Mud. Don't make new mud holes or enlarge existing ones. Stay home if you have reason to believe the trail will be too wet. Some trails, however, have permanent mud holes that you must cross. Mud can build up suction around your tires and be very difficult to get through. Always check a mud hole carefully to see how deep it is. Take a stick and poke around. Check the other side. If there are no tracks coming out, don't go in. If you decide to cross, keep moving at a steady pace and if necessary, turn the steering wheel back and forth quickly for additional traction. If you get stuck, dig around the tires to break the suction and place anything hard under the tires for traction. It may be necessary to back out. If you are with a friend, and you are doubtful if you can get through without help, attach a tow strap before you enter so that you can be pulled back. But beware, sometimes the mud can be so bad, even a friend can't pull you out. Your only protection against this happening is to use your head and not go in the mud in the first place. When I've seen people stuck this badly it is usually due to a total disregard for the obvious.

If you can't get though the mud, search for an alternate route but don't widen the trail. If there is no alternate route, turn around.

Ruts. If you get stuck in a rut and have no one to pull you out, dig a small trench from the rut to the right or left at a 45 degree angle. The dirt you remove from this trench should be used to fill the rut ahead of the turning point. If both tires are in parallel ruts, make sure the trenches are parallel. Drive out following the new rut. Repair any damage after you get out.

Gullies or washouts. If you are running parallel to a washed out section of the trail, straddle it. If it becomes too large to straddle, drive down the middle. The goal is to center your vehicle so you remain as level as possible. This may require that you drive on the outer edges of your tires, so drive slowly and watch for any sharp objects. If you begin to tilt too far in one direction, turn in the direction of the tilt until you level out again. Sometimes it helps to have a spotter. To cross a gully from one side to the other, approach at a 45-degree angle and let each tire walk over independently.

Ravines. Crossing a ravine is similar to crossing a gully. Approach on an angle and let each tire go through independently. If the ravine is large with steep sides, you may not be able to cross at an angle because it could cause a rollover. If you don't cross at an angle, two things can happen. You will drag the front or rear of your vehicle, or you will high center on the edge of the ravine. If this is the case, ask yourself if you really need to cross the ravine. If you must cross, your only solution is to stack rocks to lift the vehicle at critical points.

Sand. Except for the North Sand Hills (Trail #1) and the Great Sand Dunes National Monument, Colorado has few desert areas. Sandy soil situations are mostly encountered around dry creek beds. Not all sand is a problem. Some can be quite firm and easy to drive over. Unfortunately, you can never be sure until you are in the middle of it. The trick is to keep moving so that your momentum helps carry you through. Stay in a higher gear and use a little extra power but don't use excessive power and spin your tires. If necessary, turn your steering wheel back and forth quickly to give your tires a fresh grip. Airing down your tires can also help. Experiment with different tire pressures. Some tires can go as low as 8 to 10 pounds, although use caution below 15 pounds. Make sure you have a way to air up after you get through the sand. If you do get stuck, wet the sand in front of your tires. Try rocking the vehicle. If necessary, use your floor mats under the tires.

Snow and ice. The best advice is to avoid snow and ice completely. Call ahead for trail conditions. (See appendix.) If you encounter ice or snow on a shelf road, use extreme caution. If it is drifted over and there are no tire tracks, turn around. If other vehicles have safely crossed and there is some melting to the dirt surface, it is probably all right to cross provided you feel comfortable and have proper tires. If you are not sure, get out of your vehicle and walk the route. Be careful late in the day as the road surface may be in the process of refreezing. If you encounter any place where ice is completely across the trail, turn around.

If you are starting down a slope that is snow covered or icy, go slowly until you have some idea of how slippery the surface is. Some snow can have relatively good traction. Other snow can be too slippery to walk across. If you find your vehicle sliding, steer in the direction of the slide. Pump your brakes lightly so your wheels do not lock. This will allow your wheels to turn a little which will give you some steering capability. Don't pump antilock brakes.

Use extreme caution before starting up a slippery grade. If the road surface is off-camber, you may slide off the road. If you find yourself losing traction, try turning your steering wheel back and forth quickly for a fresh grip.

If you get stuck in the snow, dig around the tire and rock your vehicle back and forth. Try shoveling some fresh dirt, gravel, or small rocks into the hole. If no other alternative, try putting your floor mats under the tires. Don't spin your tires.

Tire chains. Many of the situations described above can be eliminated with the use of tire chains, which I recommend you carry at all times. Learn how to put them on before you need them. Chains should be properly fitted to your vehicle because they can cause damage to wheel wells or steering mechanisms.

Dust and washboard roads. Dust and washboard roads are a part of Colorado travel. Vibration from these roads can be annoying. It is a problem for everybody so don't think there is something wrong with your vehicle. Experiment with different speeds to find the smoothest ride. Slowing down is usually best, but some conditions may be improved by speeding up a little. Be careful around curves where you could lose traction and slide. Check your tires to make sure they are not over inflated. Dust is less of a problem for closed SUVs. You simply roll up your windows and turn on the air conditioner or fan. The inside pressure will help keep out most dust. With an open vehicle, there is not much you can do. At slow speeds, you can fold down your windshield if you have this option. The dust will pass through rather than collect behind the windshield.

Thumbs up. Make a habit of not wrapping your thumbs inside the steering wheel when crossing over rocky terrain. If you hit a large rock, your steering wheel could spin suddenly and injure your thumbs. This is more of a problem for vehicles without power steering.

Airing down. There may be times when you need to let air out of your tires to get more traction or improve your ride, e.g., when driving through sand, going up a steep hill, or driving on washboard roads. It is usually safe to let air out of your tires until they bulge slightly, provided you are not traveling at high speed. If you let out too much air, your tires may come off the rims, or the sidewalls may become vulnerable to damage by sharp objects. Consider how or where you will reinflate. A small air pump that plugs into your cigarette lighter is handy for this purpose. Airing down on hard-core trails is essential. I've seen some wheelers with larger tires air down to as little as 3-5 lbs. A typical SUV can usually be aired down to 18 to 20 lbs. without noticeable handling difficulties at low speeds.

Winching. Next to tow points and skid plates, a winch is one of the best investments you can make. If you drive more difficult trails and you don't have a winch, travel with someone who does. I've known some hard-core wheelers who have gone for years without owning a winch but they always travel with a group. If you never intend to buy a winch, carry a high lift jack or come-along. Although these tools are slow and inconvenient, they can get you out of difficulty when there is no other way.

If you own a winch, make sure you also have these four basic winch accessories:

1. Heavy-duty work gloves.

2. A tree strap - Looks like a tow strap but is shorter. It has a loop on each end.

3. A snatch block - A pulley that opens on the side so you can slip it over your winch cable.

4. A clevis - A heavy U-shaped device with a pin that screws across one end. This enables you to connect straps together and to your vehicle. It has many other uses.

Winching tips:

• Your winch cable should be lined up straight with the pulling vehicle. If you can't pull straight, attach a snatch block to a tree to form an angle. This technique also works for pulling a fallen tree off the trail.

• If your winch cable bunches up at one end of the spool, let it go and rewind the cable later.

• Attach your winch line to the largest tree possible using your tree strap and clevis. If no tree is large enough, wrap several smaller trees. The strap should be put as low as possible on the tree.

• Keep your engine running while winching to provide maximum electrical power to the battery.

• Help the winch by driving the stuck vehicle slowly. Be in the lowest gear possible and go as slowly as possible. Don't allow slack in the winch cable. This can start a jerking motion that could break the cable.

• If there is not enough power to pull the stuck vehicle, attach a snatch block to the stuck vehicle and double the winch cable back to the starting point. This block-and-tackle technique will double your pulling power.

• Set the emergency brake on the anchor vehicle and block the wheels if necessary. In some cases, you may have to connect the anchor vehicle to another vehicle or tree.

• Throw a blanket or heavy coat over the winch cable while pulling. This will slow the end of the winch cable if it breaks and snaps back.

• Make sure there are at least 5 wraps of the winch cable left on the spool.

• Never hook the winch cable to itself. Use a tree strap and clevis. Never allow the winch cable to kink. This creates a weak spot in the cable.

• If tow points are not available on the stuck vehicle, attach the winch cable to the frame not the bumper. If you are helping a stranger, make sure he understands that you are not responsible for damage to his vehicle.

• Never straddle or stand close to the winch cable while it is under stress.

• If you are stuck alone with no place to attach your winch cable, bury your spare tire in the ground as an anchor point. When you are finished, repair any damage to the ground.

• When finished winching, don't let the end of the cable wind into the spool. It can become jammed and damage your winch. Attach the hook to some other part of your vehicle like a tow point.

OTHER ACTIVITIES

To make the trip more enjoyable for everyone, especially if children are along, plan frequent stops with a variety of activities including picnics, hiking, biking, camping, rafting, and fishing. Go to the library before your trip and learn a little history about the area or stop at museums in towns along the way. Share maps with the kids and let them trace your route. Carry binoculars to look for wildlife and distant landmarks. Allow your adult passengers an opportunity to drive appropriate parts of the trail if they are so inclined. Some portions of the trail provide driving opportunities for responsible licensed teenagers. They will be eager to learn proper off-highway driving techniques and will grow up to be responsible adult backcountry drivers.

FINAL COMMENTS

I've made every effort to make this book as accurate and as easy to use as possible. If you have ideas for improvements or find any significant errors, please write to me at FunTreks, Inc., P.O. Box 49187, Colorado Springs, CO. 80949-9187. Or, send E Mail to: *funtreks@pcisys.net*. In addition, I would love to hear stories of your travels. Whether you're a novice or expert, I hope this book has made your backcountry experience safer, easier, and more fun.

Map Legend

Interstate

Paved Road*

Easy Trail*

Moderate Trail*

Difficult Trail*

Other Road*

Described in text

Hiking Trail

Boundaries, & Divides

Mountain

Lake

Map Orientation

Pass Locator

Interstate

U.S. Highway

State & County Road

Forest Service Road

Trail Closed

Starting point of trail description

Public Toilet

Gas, Service

Parking

Picnic Area

Camping Area

Mine or Mill

Hiking Trailhead

Mountain Biking

Fishing

Water Crossing

Bridge

Falls

Cabin

Ghost Town

Scenic Point

Major Obstacle

Handicap Access

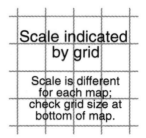

Scale indicated by grid

Scale is different for each map; check grid size at bottom of map.

These items repeated on each map for your convenience. See Mini Key.

THE TRAILS

Kelly Flats, Trail #3, Difficult.

Fort Collins, Loveland, Walden

1. North Sand Hills
2. Sevenmile Road 225
3. Kelly Flats
4. Green Ridge Road
5. Old Flowers Road
6. Ballard Road
7. Moody Hill
8. Crystal Mountain
9. Storm Mountain

EASY

MODERATE

DIFFICULT

N

MINI KEY
- Paved
- Easy
- Moderate
- Difficult
- Other

Grid size - 10 miles

Cowdrey

Glendevey

Walden

Red Feather Lakes

The Forks

Livermore

Rustic

Poudre Park

Teds Place

LaPorte

Ft. Collins

Horsetooth Reservoir

Masonville

Loveland

Berthoud

Lyons

Raymond

Longmont

Cameron Pass

Gould

Rand

Trail Ridge Road

Rocky Mountain National Park

Grand Lake

Lake Granby

Glen Haven

Drake

Estes Park

25, 14, 68, 287, 56, 1, 34, 27, 38E, 52E, 54G, 44H, 43, 36, 66, 7, 162, 68C, 63E, 74E, 103, 125, 6

Fort Collins, Loveland, Walden

Many of the trails in this area are reached by traveling through the beautiful Cache La Poudre River Valley on State Route 14. This valley provides spectacular scenery and many recreational activities including four-wheeling, hiking, biking, fishing, rafting and kayaking. World class rapids can be found on a well-known section of the river called the *Narrows*, which can be seen from the highway. There are numerous Forest Service campgrounds and picnic areas along the way. Solitude can be found in the nearby Cache La Poudre Wilderness, Comanche Park Wilderness, and Rawah Wilderness. South of this area, and west of Loveland, Trail #9 climbs to Storm Mountain. From there, one can see Rocky Mountain National Park and the front range simultaneously. The best known hard-core four-wheel drive trail in the area is Kelly Flats (Trail #3) which serves up one of the toughest obstacles in the state. Called the *Chutes,* it is a diabolically narrow stretch that challenges the most serious four-wheeler. Northeast of Walden, air down your tires and frolic in the sand with dune buggies and ATVs at the North Sand Hills Recreation Area (Trail #1). Here, winds crossing the Medicine Bow Mountains have formed a minidesert.

Lower Storm Mountain (Trail #9) is easy with nice views of Rocky Mountain National Park.

33

Banked turn on one of the larger dunes.

Air down your tires to get through the sand.

Watch for dune buggies and ATVs.

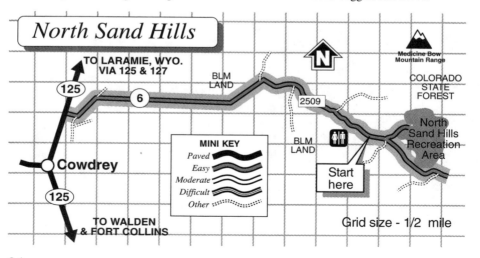

North Sand Hills

TO LARAMIE, WYO.
VIA 125 & 127

125

6

BLM
LAND

2509

BLM
LAND

N

Medicine Bow
Mountain Range

COLORADO
STATE
FOREST

North
Sand Hills
Recreation
Area

Cowdrey

125

MINI KEY
Paved
Easy
Moderate
Difficult
Other

Start
here

TO WALDEN
& FORT COLLINS

Grid size - 1/2 mile

34

North Sand Hills ❶

Location: West of Fort Collins. Southwest of Laramie, Wyoming.

Difficulty: Easy. Gently rolling hills of sand mixed with patches of brush. Air down your tires to perhaps as low as 12 to 15 lbs to compensate for the soft sand. The sand creates extra resistance and could cause your engine to overheat if you get too aggressive, so watch your temperature guage.

Features: Provides an opportunity to drive in desert-like terrain.

Time & Distance: Allow about 2 1/2 hours driving time to reach the North Sand Hills Recreation Area from Fort Collins. It's about 115 miles one way. Time passes quickly during this beautiful drive through the Cache La Poudre River Valley and over Cameron Pass (10,276 ft.). Once at the recreation area, spend as much time as you like exploring. I found 2 to 3 hours sufficient. Pack a picnic lunch and allow a full day with return time.

To Get There: From the north side of Fort Collins, take State Rt. 14 west to Walden. Head north through Walden on Rt. 125. Soon after passing through Cowdrey, turn right on County Rd. 6. Follow the main part of this wide gravel road about 3 miles, then turn right on a narrow sandy road marked #2509. Signs mark the recreation area which you should be able to see ahead of you. You'll pass through a gate; close it behind you. From this point the sand gets softer. You'll need to air down about 3 miles from County Rd. 6. Experiment with tire pressure since every vehicle is different.

Trail Description: No directions are necessary at the hills. Drive just about anywhere unless posted. Stay out of areas that are roped-off. Use common sense at all times. More challenge is available on the southeast side where the dunes slope steeply into North Sand Creek.

Return Trip: Return the way you came or take Routes 125 and 127 northeast to Laramie, Wyo. From there take I-80/I-25 or 287 back to Fort Collins.

Services: A pit toilet is at the area. Full services in Walden.

Other Activities: Picnicking and open camping. Motor homes are allowed.

Maps: Trails Illustrated Cowdrey, North Sand Hills #113, Colorado Atlas and Gazetteer.

There are numerous water crossings and muddy spots.

Open meadow near end of trail.

The trail is narrow in spots.

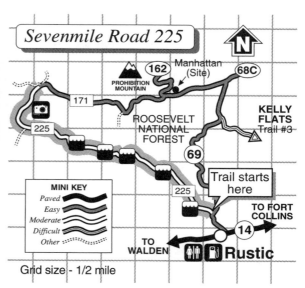

Sevenmile Road 225

N

PROHIBITION MOUNTAIN

(162)

Manhattan (Site)

(68C)

171

KELLY FLATS
Trail #3

225

ROOSEVELT NATIONAL FOREST

(69)

225

Trail starts here

MINI KEY
Paved
Easy
Moderate
Difficult
Other

TO FORT COLLINS

(14)

TO WALDEN

Rustic

Grid size - 1/2 mile

Sevenmile Road 225

Location: West of Fort Collins in the Cache La Poudre River Valley.

Difficulty: Moderate. Several rocky sections require careful driving and tire placement. Skid plates are recommended. Shallow water crossings may be deeper in the spring. Overgrown trees and brush create narrow spots along the way. Branches may scrape the sides of your vehicle.

Features: The trail crosses Sevenmile Creek many times and climbs to a high point at the end. Spur roads link to more difficult trails.

Time & Distance: The trail itself is about 5 miles long and takes 1 to 2 hours. Add another 1/2 hour to return to Highway 14.

To Get There: Take Highway 14 west from Fort Collins about 40 miles. Just before the town of Rustic, turn right and head uphill on County Rd. 69 following signs to Boy Scout Camp. Go 0.4 miles to Sevenmile Road 225 on the left.

Trail Description: Reset your odometer at the start. The trail starts as a wide gravel road but quickly narrows. After a gate, bear left where you'll drop down into a wet, rocky spot. Tree limbs may brush against your vehicle. From this point forward, you cross the creek many times. Bear left at 1.1 miles and 1.7 miles. Several undulating muddy sections follow. Go slow and place your tires carefully. Use a spotter if necessary. Bear right after a meadow at 4 miles. If looking for a diversion, a spur road to the left of the meadow takes you through a deep water hole to a difficult area. At 4.1, bear left at a cabin as you start climbing. At 5.2, the trail ends at the top of a hill and is followed by a spaghetti-work of roads with no markings.

Return Trip: Bear right through the spaghetti-work until F.S. 171 becomes obvious. After about 2 miles, you reach F.S. 162. Turn right. In another mile, turn right again on County Rd. 69. This road was not marked. If you go straight, you end up on 68C. Rustic is about 3.2 miles down the hill on County Rd. 69. You'll pass the west end of Kelly Flats (Trail #3).

Services: A little store with gas and restrooms is located in Rustic.

Maps: Trails Illustrated Poudre River, Cameron Pass #112, Roosevelt National Forest, Colorado Atlas and Gazetteer.

Between the challenging obstacles, Kelly Flats is a scenic and relaxing drive.

Group prepares to go up *Heart Attack Hill*.

Part way through the difficult *Chutes*.

Heart Attack Hill is long, steep, and rocky.

Entering the *Chutes*.

38

Kelly Flats ◀ 3 ▶

Location: West of Fort Collins in the Cache La Poudre River Valley.

Difficulty: Difficult. One of the premier hard-core trails in Northern Colorado. Differential lockers and high ground clearance are required. Body damage possible getting through the *Chutes*.

Features: The trail climbs steeply out of the Poudre River Valley and winds for a considerable distance across a high ridge affording beautiful views of the Mummy Mountain Range on a clear day. Noted obstacles include the *Chutes* and *Heart Attack Hill*. This trail is normally closed mid November to late May.

Time & Distance: The trail is just under 11 miles long. It can be driven in a couple of hours if you rush, but I would allow 3 to 4 hours. Add additional time if you are traveling with a group.

To Get There: Take the Highway 287 bypass around LaPorte north of Fort Collins. Drive about 6 miles and turn left on Hwy. 14 at Teds Place, a large gas station and popular stop. Kelly Flats is another 25 miles. Watch for a parking area on the right after the Kelly Flats Forest Service Campground. There are no toilet facilities at the trailhead. Kelly Flats is F.S. Road 168.

Trail Description: *Reset your odometer at the start of the trail.* There's a rough section immediately as you pass through a gate. Bear left at 0.4 miles. At 0.6 miles go straight or left for *Heart Attack Hill*. A bypass goes to the right here. It is fairly long and still pretty challenging. Engage your lockers for *Heart Attack Hill*. It's steep and rocky. At 1.7 miles bear left as the bypass rejoins the trail on the right. As you climb, enjoy beautiful views of the Mummy Mountain Range to the south. Looking carefully, you can see the image of a mummy lying on its back.

   The trail splits several times and rejoins itself. At 3.0 miles, a sign indicates you are crossing private land. Please pass through quietly and respect the rights of the property owners. Bear left at 3.1 miles, continuing on F.S. 168. Bear left again at 3.7 miles staying on the well-graded private road. At 4.7 miles, you leave private land and the road gets rough again. You will drop down into a rutted area that is very tight between the trees. At 5.1 miles turn right sharply. A lesser road dead ends if you go straight. You reach the *Chutes* at 5.4 miles—a good point to stop for lunch. At the time of this writing, there was a bypass around the *Chutes* to the right. (See Special

Note at the bottom of this page.) I'd recommend taking a close look at the *Chutes* before entering. You may have to turn around if you are not properly equipped. At 6.0 a couple of obstacles can be bypassed. Scout ahead and select the path most suitable for you. Bear left at 6.7 miles. At 7.1 a fun stretch climbs through a washed-out area with big moguls. At 7.5 miles you pass through a large pit that may contain water.

The next 3.3 miles are uneventful as you pass through an easy but attractive area called Wintersteen Park. This is the highest point of the trail at about 8,700 ft. This part of the trail is easy when starting from the other end. The trail ends as you pass through a gate at 10.8 miles.

Return Trip: Turn left on Pingree Hill Road County Rd. 69 and head downhill 2.4 miles to paved Highway 14 near the town of Rustic. You will pass the entrance to Sevenmile Road 225 (Trail #2) about 2 miles down County Rd. 69. Turn left at Highway 14 to get back to Fort Collins.

Services: Public toilets at the Kelly Flats F.S. Campground prior to reaching the trail. Gas and restrooms are available in Rustic.

Other Activities: The western end of the trail, when dry, is ideal for mountain biking. Other activities are mentioned in the introduction to this area.

Maps: Roosevelt National Forest, the Colorado Atlas and Gazetteer. This trail is shown on two Trails Illustrated maps. The eastern end of the trail is on Cache La Poudre, Big Thompson #101. The western end of the trail is on Poudre River, Cameron Pass #112.

Special Note: At the time of this writing, Kelly Flats trail is scheduled for road improvement in the Chutes area to access private land. This road construction will take out a small challenge at 5.2 miles and the bypass around the Chutes. Members of the Larimer County Mountaineers (the four-wheel drive club in Fort Collins) have been working closely with the Forest Service. They have been assured that the Chutes and Heart Attack Hill will remain a challenge route as will most of the rest of the Kelly Flats trail.

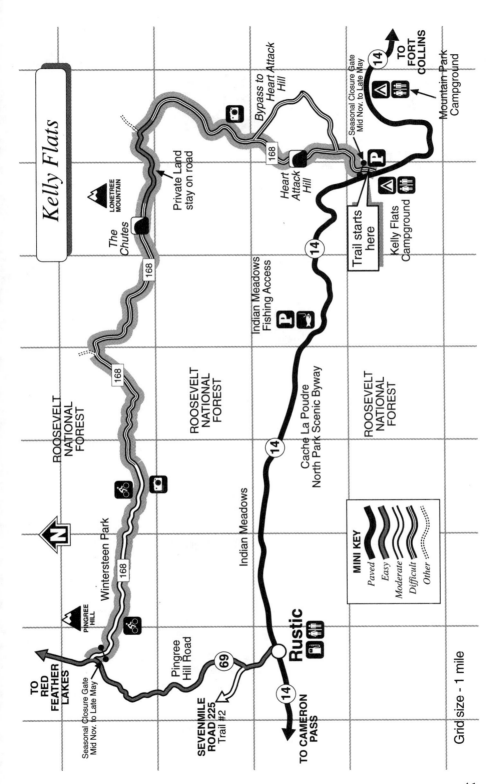

Kelly Flats

LONETREE MOUNTAIN

The Chutes

Private Land stay on road

168

Bypass to Heart Attack Hill

168

Heart Attack Hill

Seasonal Closure Gate Mid Nov. to Late May

P

Mountain Park Campground

TO FORT COLLINS

14

Kelly Flats Campground

Trail starts here

14

Indian Meadows Fishing Access

P

ROOSEVELT NATIONAL FOREST

ROOSEVELT NATIONAL FOREST

ROOSEVELT NATIONAL FOREST

168

168

Cache La Poudre North Park Scenic Byway

14

Wintersteen Park

168

N

PINGREE HILL

Indian Meadows

Pingree Hill Road

Seasonal Closure Gate Mid Nov. to Late May

TO RED FEATHER LAKES

69

SEVENMILE ROAD 225 Trail #2

Rustic

14

TO CAMERON PASS

MINI KEY

Paved
Easy
Moderate
Difficult
Other

Grid size - 1 mile

We assembled at the trailhead on October 4. The day started with a surprise wet snowfall.

A tow strap was required to get out of this nasty spot.

Starting into the *Long Trough*.

Much of the trail looks like this.

Green Ridge Road ◀4▶

Location: West of Fort Collins. North of Cameron Pass.

Difficulty: Difficult. This trail is very muddy with several extremely long water troughs. They can be very deep in the spring or after heavy rains. Hidden under the water are large rocks, tree stumps, and unknown surprises. Two vehicles in our group knocked tires off rims or broke tire seals. If you get stuck in the deepest part of one of these troughs, your vehicle will likely fill with black, smelly water. The trail is not as bad during the drier summer months, but water and mud are always present. The trail is fairly flat, gradually rising and falling between 9,500 ft. and 10,000 ft. Expect more frequent snows at this high altitude. When we ran the trail on Oct.4, it snowed all day accumulating about 3 inches. Mileages may vary significantly because of differences in tire spinning.

Features: Fishing is allowed at Lost Lake, near the start of the trail. Several other small lakes can be seen along the way. Insect repellent is recommended during the warmer months. Much of the trail is shaded by dense trees and is not particularly scenic.

Time & Distance: The route described here covers a distance of 19 miles. Our group took over 5 hours to complete the trip, however, we stopped about 1 1/2 hours to fix tires. We exited the trail at the first opportunity at Nunn Creek Rd. F.S. 319. If you continue forward and exit at Killpecker Road F.S. 300, it adds another 5 or 6 miles.You can go even farther by taking Elkhorn Baldy Road 517 all the way to Manhattan Road, which takes you north to Red Feather Lakes. Consult additional maps listed at the end of the next page.

To Get There: Take the Hwy. 287 bypass around LaPorte north of Fort Collins. Drive about 6 miles and turn left on Hwy. 14 at Teds Place, a large gas station and popular stop. Go another 45 miles to County Rd. 103. Turn right following a sign to Laramie, Wyo. Go about 1.6 miles and turn right again. Drive a short distance to a parking area. The trail is on the right and is marked as F.S. 177.

Trail Description: Reset your odometer at the parking area as you start down the trail. Bear to the right at 0.1 miles. At 0.4 miles Lost Lake can be seen through the trees on the right. Bear right again at 0.5 miles. The orange signs on the trees are for snowmobilers. The first muddy section is reached at 1.4 miles, which is followed by the *Long Trough* at 1.7 miles. This obstacle is about as long as a football field and wide enough for one vehicle. It is a difficult, messy job to reach someone with a winch if they get stuck in the trough. The water was about 3 feet deep when our group went through. Large rocks under the water toss you around, but you are just as likely to get stuck if you try to drive around the troughs. I recommend you drive this trail in the drier part of summer to avoid these worst-case conditions. After the *Long Trough*, it gets better, but many muddy, wet sections follow.

At 11.8 miles, you enter a meadow and pass through a gate. To exit on Nunn Creek Rd. F.S. 319 as we did, take the left fork across the meadow following F.S. 177A. You immediately go back into the trees on the other side of the meadow. There may have been another road to the left before entering the trees, but we couldn't see it under the snow. If so, ignore it. You reach a good road at 12.1. Bear right; a closed gate is to the left. At 13.6, you cross Nunn Creek. Bear left at 17.9 and go straight at 18.3. You reach Deadman Road 162 at 18.9 miles.

Return Trip: Bear right on Deadman Rd. 162. The town of Red Feather Lakes is about 13 miles. From there the road becomes paved and is marked as County Rd. 74E which takes you to US 287. At 287, right takes you to Fort Collins and left takes you to Laramie, Wyo.

Services: There is a modern pit toilet at the start of the trail but no other services until Red Feather Lakes.

Other Activities: Camping is available on Chambers Lake just past the turn-off for 103. Fishing is permitted at Lost Lake at the start of the trail. This is a popular area for snowmobiles in the winter.

Maps: Trails Illustrated Red Feather Lakes, Glendevey #111 and Poudre River, Cameron Pass #112, Roosevelt National Forest, Colorado Atlas and Gazetteer.

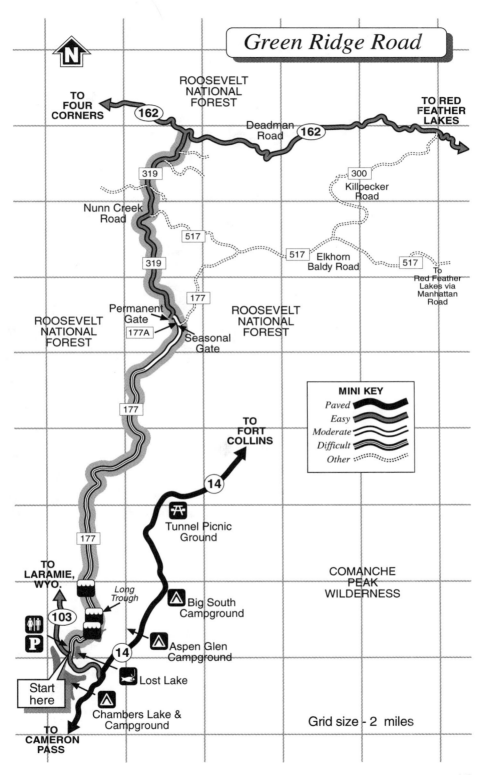

Green Ridge Road

N

ROOSEVELT NATIONAL FOREST

TO FOUR CORNERS

162

Deadman Road 162

TO RED FEATHER LAKES

319

300
Killpecker Road

Nunn Creek Road

517

319

517 Elkhorn Baldy Road

517

To Red Feather Lakes via Manhattan Road

177

Permanent Gate

177A

ROOSEVELT NATIONAL FOREST

ROOSEVELT NATIONAL FOREST

Seasonal Gate

177

MINI KEY

Paved
Easy
Moderate
Difficult
Other

TO FORT COLLINS

14

Tunnel Picnic Ground

177

COMANCHE PEAK WILDERNESS

TO LARAMIE, WYO.

Long Trough

Big South Campground

103

Aspen Glen Campground

14

Lost Lake

Start here

Chambers Lake & Campground

Grid size - 2 miles

TO CAMERON PASS

The start of Old Flowers Road on the eastern end crosses private property.

In the National Forest, camping is allowed near the road unless posted otherwise.

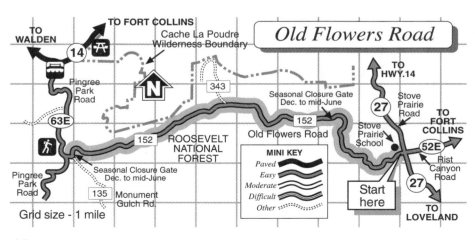

Old Flowers Road

TO WALDEN

TO FORT COLLINS

TO FORT COLLINS

Cache La Poudre Wilderness Boundary

14

N

Pingree Park Road

63E

343

152

Seasonal Closure Gate Dec. to mid-June

152

Old Flowers Road

ROOSEVELT NATIONAL FOREST

152

Seasonal Closure Gate Dec. to mid-June

Pingree Park Road

135 Monument Gulch Rd.

Grid size - 1 mile

MINI KEY

Paved
Easy
Moderate
Difficult
Other

TO HWY.14

27

Stove Prairie Road

Stove Prairie School

TO FORT COLLINS

52E

Rist Canyon Road

Start here

27

TO LOVELAND

Old Flowers Road ⑤

Location: West of Fort Collins through Rist Canyon.

Difficulty: Easy. Portions can get a little muddy after a heavy rain.

Features: A relaxing drive through the forest and not far from town.

Time & Distance: Just under 12 miles. Takes about 1 hour without stops. Allow half a day to get there and return to Fort Collins.

To Get There: From Fort Collins, head west on Highway 14 into LaPorte. Hwy. 14 becomes County Rd. 54G. A short distance after going through LaPorte, turn left following signs to Rist Canyon on County Rd. 52E. After passing through Bellvue, the road winds through Rist Canyon about 13 miles until it intersects with Stove Prairie Road County Rd. 27. Continue straight to Old Flowers Road. Stove Prairie School is on the right.

Trail Description: Reset your odometer at the start. Bear left at 0.6 miles and right at 0.8 miles. Turns are well marked. At 1.8 miles, you pass through a private homestead. Leave all gates the way you found them. Be quiet and respect the rights of property owners. Bear right at 2.7 miles and right again at 3.0 miles. You reach the Forest Gate at 3.4 miles and the road becomes F.S. 152. The gate is seasonally closed between December and mid-June. The road becomes mogully so you may need four-wheel drive under wet conditions. Go straight at 4.9 miles, as 152B goes right. Pass through another gate at 5.2 miles. At 6.7 miles 152C goes left; you go straight. At 8.5 veer a little left as F.S. 236 goes to the right. Minor spurs continue to intersect. Follow the main part of the road until the trail ends at 11.8 miles at a gate.

Return Trip: Bear right after the last gate and go a short distance on Monument Gulch Rd. F.S 135 before intersecting with Pingree Park Road 63E. Turn right and follow 63E to Highway 14 on a 7.7 mile drive through a beautiful canyon. Right at Hwy. 14 takes you back to Fort Collins in about 36 miles.

Services: Gas is available in LaPorte and several places on Highway 14.

Maps: Trails Illustrated maps #101 and #112, Roosevelt National Forest, Colorado Atlas and Gazetteer.

You pass through aspen groves that are colorful in the fall.

Park and hike to Donner Pass. Trails eventually connect to Rocky Mountain National Park.

First part of the road is easy.

Ballard Road [6]

Location: West of Fort Collins on the western end of Buckhorn Canyon.

Difficulty: Moderate. The lower portion of the road is easy. The upper portion becomes narrower and rockier. Branches will brush against your vehicle if you go up far enough. There are numerous spur roads.

Features: This trail is open all year and makes a good winter trip if snow-covered. Provides access to the Donner Pass Hiking Trail.

Time & Distance: The trail is about 6 miles long, if you go up as far as possible. Allow about an hour one way.

To Get There: From Fort Collins, follow directions to Old Flowers Road (Trail # 5). When you get to Old Flowers Road turn south and take Stove Prairie Rd. 27 about 4 miles to Buckhorn Rd 44H. Head west on Buckhorn Road 10.2 miles to Ballard Road F.S. 129 on the left. From Loveland, head west on Hwy. 34 to County Rd 27. Go north to Masonville and bear left. Continue on 27 to Buckhorn Road 44H on the left.

Trail Description: Reset your odometer at the start of the trail. Bear right at 0.2 miles and left at 1.0 miles. At 1.2 miles Greer Road goes right, you bear left. You reach the Donner Pass Hiking Trail at 2.8 miles with a parking area at the trailhead. At 4.0 miles, bear left. The road gets steeper and narrower. At some point, you'll want to shift into four-wheel drive. Bear right at 5.2 and again at 5.3 miles. I turned around at 5.8 miles as the road tapered down to a narrow ATV trail, although I probably could have pushed my way through the trees a little farther.

Return Trip: Return the way you came or head west on Buckhorn Road 44H to Pingree Park Road 63E. Take 63E north to Hwy. 14. Turn right on 14 to get back to Fort Collins.

Services: Return to Fort Collins or head south to Masonville on Cty. Rd. 27.

Other Activities: Hike up to Donner Pass or down to the Buckhorn Ranger Station. Picnic at several places along Buckhorn Road.

Maps: Trails Illustrated Cache La Poudre, Big Thompson #101, Roosevelt National Forest, Colorado Atlas and Gazetteer.

Road is steep but smooth at this point.

Rear tire loses traction on this steep section.

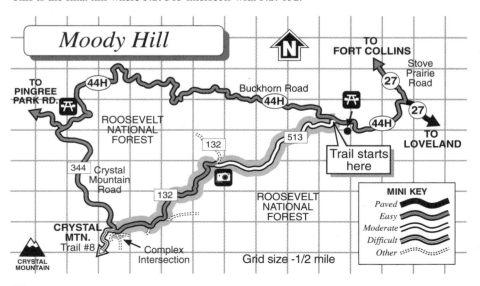
This is the final hill where F.S. 513 intersects with F.S. 132.

Moody Hill 7

Location: West of Fort Collins on the eastern end of Buckhorn Canyon.

Difficulty: Moderate. One of the more challenging moderate trails. The first part of the trail is steep with some fairly large moguls. If you're not sure of your driving skills, you may want to inspect the first part of the trail on foot. High ground clearance and good articulation are recommended.

Features: A short drive from Fort Collins. Offers exciting challenges to the more adventurous sport utility owner. A fun way to reach the start of Crystal Mountain (Trail #8).

Time & Distance: About 5 miles long. Allow 1 to 1 1/2 hours to go up.

To Get There: From Fort Collins, follow directions to Old Flowers Road (Trail # 5). At Old Flowers Road, turn left on Stove Prairie Road 27. Go about 4 miles south and turn right on Buckhorn Road 44H. The trail is on the left 1.6 miles west on Buckhorn Road. It is marked as F.S. 513.

C PENCOCK PASS

Trail Description: Reset your odometer at the start. The trail starts climbing immediately. The steepest part is at the beginning. Within 0.2 miles, a side road leads to a mining area. You bear left. At 1.1 miles, bear left again as 513A goes right. At 1.6 miles, bear right as 513B goes left. After leveling off a little, you reach a meadow at 2.3 miles. Cross the meadow and climb a hill. At the top of the hill, at 2.9 miles, you run into F.S. 132. It dead-ends to the right. Turn left as the road levels out and improves. You pass through a gate at 3.8 miles. The trail ends at 5.1 miles at a complex intersection where it meets Crystal Mountain Road.

Return Trip: To end the trip, turn right and head downhill on Crystal Mountain Road. You'll reach Buckhorn Road in 2.4 miles. Turn right to return to Fort Collins. To continue the trip up the difficult part of Crystal Mountain (Trail #8), go straight at the complex intersection.

Services: Closest services are back to La Porte and Fort Collins. Eat at a restaurant in Masonville if you are heading back to Loveland.

Maps: Trails Illustrated Cache La Poudre, Big Thompson #101, Roosevelt National Forest, Colorado Atlas and Gazetteer.

This obstacle is encountered early.

Relaxing at the top with views in all directions.

This section is extremely steep & loose.

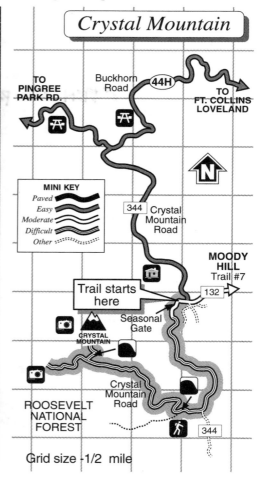

Crystal Mountain

TO PINGREE PARK RD.

Buckhorn Road

44H

TO FT. COLLINS LOVELAND

N

MINI KEY
Paved
Easy
Moderate
Difficult
Other

344 Crystal Mountain Road

MOODY HILL Trail #7

132

Trail starts here

Seasonal Gate

CRYSTAL MOUNTAIN

Crystal Mountain Road

ROOSEVELT NATIONAL FOREST

344

Grid size -1/2 mile

Crystal Mountain ◆8

Location: West of Fort Collins on the south side of Buckhorn Canyon.

Difficulty: Difficult. Most obstacles are not extremely difficult by hard-core standards, however, the final climb to the top is very steep with large loose rocks and moguls. Lockers are recommended for this section.

Features: Great views from the top of Crystal Mountain (Elev. 9,949 ft.).

Time & Distance: The top of Crystal Mountain is 4 miles from the starting point shown on the map. Allow about 3 hours for the round trip.

To Get There: The most interesting way to reach the start of the trail is to first complete Moody Hill (Trail #7). It ends at Crystal Mountain Road at the starting point shown on the map.

A faster but less interesting way is to drive up Crystal Mountain Road 2.4 miles direct from Buckhorn Road 44H. To find Buckhorn Road, follow directions to Old Flowers Road (Trail #5). When you reach Old Flowers Road, head south on Stove Prairie Road about 4 miles. Drive 8.4 miles west on Buckhorn Road to Crystal Mountain Road on the left.

Trail Description: *Reset your odometer at the start.* Pass through a seasonal gate at 0.1 miles. Continue straight as another road joins at 1.5 miles. At 1.8, bear right. At 2.1, bear right again for the first obstacle. Several closed spurs go left. Continue right on the main part of the road. Watch for a steep hill to the right at 3.8 miles that takes you to the top. This section is very steep and challenging and requires great articulation or lockers. At 3.9 miles, bear left. The end of this part of the trail is at 4.0 miles. When you get back down to the bottom of this tough section, turn right to the end of the trail or go left to return to the bottom.

Return Trip: Return the way you came or head west on Buckhorn Road 44H to Pingree Park Road 63E. Take 63E north to Hwy. 14.

Services: Return to Fort Collins or head south to Masonville on Cty. Rd. 27.

Other Activities: Hike to Donner Pass and Lookout Mountain.

Maps: Trails Illustrated Cache La Poudre, Big Thompson #101, Roosevelt National Forest, Colorado Atlas and Gazetteer.

Looking southeast from the summit back toward Loveland and the front range.

Longs Peak and Rocky Mountain National Park as seen from the summit.

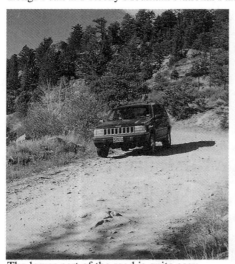

The lower part of the road is quite easy.   This difficult spot is steeper than it looks here.

54

Storm Mountain ◆ 9 ▶

Location: West of Loveland. North of Drake.

Difficulty: Difficult. This trail is rated difficult because of one small section near the top. Most of the trail is easy. If you avoid going all the way up, this trail can be enjoyed in any stock sport utility vehicle. The lower half, when dry, can be driven in a passenger car.

Features: The lower half of the trail passes through a scenic residential area before reaching the Roosevelt National Forest. Drive slowly and respect the privacy of the homeowners. Private driveways are clearly marked. Beautiful views of the front range and Rocky Mountain National Park can be seen without going all the way to the top.

Time & Distance: You reach the gate to the Roosevelt National Forest in 6.7 miles. Add another 2.5 miles to go all the way to the top. Allow about 1 hour to reach the forest boundary and an additional 1/2 hour to go all the way up.

To Get There: Head west from Loveland on US 34 to the small town of Drake. Drake is about 16 miles west of Lake Loveland. To get there, you pass through the spectacular Big Thompson Canyon. As you approach Drake, a large attractive picnic area is on the left. Just after Drake, turn right on County Rd. 43 following signs to Glen Haven. In 0.3 miles, turn right and cross a small bridge. This is Cedar Park Road and the start of the trail.

Trail Description: *Reset your odometer as you turn off County Rd. 43 and cross the small bridge.* The road twists up the hillside rather steeply on a bumpy washboard surface. Tight blind curves require careful attention. At 2.2 miles turn left continuing on F.S. 128 Storm Mountain Drive. Bear left again at 2.5 and 3.5. At 3.9 miles you can see views of the front range behind you and at 4.3 miles Rocky Mountain National Park can be seen on the left. Bear right at 5.7 miles, left at 5.8, and right again at 6.5. At 6.7 miles you reach a gate for the Roosevelt National Forest. This seasonal gate is closed when conditions are too wet. In the spring, check with the Forest Service (see Appendix) to make sure the gate is open.

At 6.9 miles F.S. 128 intersects with F.S. 153 at a place called Galuche Meadow. Storm Mountain turns to the left. You can also go right on 153, which takes you into Bear Gulch and to a network of roads. I did not explore this area, but I do know you must come back out the same way you enter. Private property blocks all exits with the exception of F.S. 345, which is open only a short time during hunting season.

To reach Galuche Meadow, turn left on F.S. 153. Bear left at 7.1 miles. As you enter the trees, the road becomes steep. Do not go up this road after a heavy rain. It is extremely difficult and damage to the road is possible. At 7.5 miles, you reach the obstacle that causes this trail to be rated difficult. A stock, high-clearance vehicle can get through, however, it will take some effort and skillful driving. Above the obstacle, it levels out until you come to another meadow at 8.5 miles. Bear right and climb a steep hill. The hill looks a little intimidating but the road surface is solid with good traction. There are a couple of moderately rocky sections. You enter the forest again before reaching the practical end of the road and a wide area to park. The views from this point on a clear day are breathtaking. To the east is Fort Collins and distinctive Horsetooth Mountain. Loveland is to the southeast. Rocky Mountain National Park and Longs Peak can be seen to the southwest. Storm Mountain is at an elevation of 9,918 ft.

Return Trip: Return the way you came.

Services: There are some services in Drake but you'll need to return to Loveland for full services. There are toilets at the Forks Park F.S. Picnic Grounds just east of Drake. Estes Park also has full services.

Other Activities: There is great hiking, fishing, camping, and picnicking at many places along Big Thompson Canyon. You may continue on County Rd. 43 into Glen Haven, which has several picnic grounds and hiking trails. Of course, you're only a short drive away from one of the premier recreational areas in the world—Rocky Mountain National Park.

Historical Highlights: On July 31, 1976, the worst natural disaster in Colorado history occurred in Big Thompson Canyon. Over ten inches of rain fell in a four hour period, a situation expected to occur only once in 100 years. As water was funnelled through the narrow canyon, it reached an estimated depth of 30 feet in places and virtually destroyed everything in its path—from Drake to the eastern end of the canyon. Much of Glen Haven was also destroyed. At least 145 people were killed and hundreds injured.

Warning: Exit the canyon at first sign of heavy rain or rising water. If you are caught in the canyon, don't try to outrun rising water. Get out of your vehicle and climb to safety up the canyon walls.

Maps: Trails Illustrated Cache La Poudre, Big Thompson #101, Roosevelt National Forest, Colorado Atlas and Gazetteer.

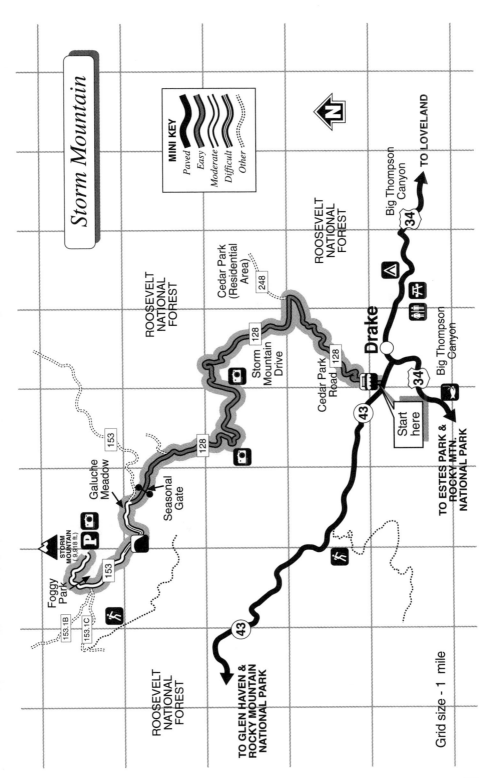

Storm Mountain

MINI KEY
Paved
Easy
Moderate
Difficult
Other

N

TO LOVELAND

Big Thompson Canyon

34

ROOSEVELT NATIONAL FOREST

Cedar Park (Residential Area)

248

ROOSEVELT NATIONAL FOREST

128

Storm Mountain Drive

Drake

128

Cedar Park Road

128

34

Big Thompson Canyon

Start here

43

TO ESTES PARK & ROCKY MTN. NATIONAL PARK

153

Galuche Meadow

Seasonal Gate

128

STORM MOUNTAIN (9,918 ft.)

P

Foggy Park

153

153.1B
153.1C

ROOSEVELT NATIONAL FOREST

43

TO GLEN HAVEN & ROCKY MOUNTAIN NATIONAL PARK

Grid size - 1 mile

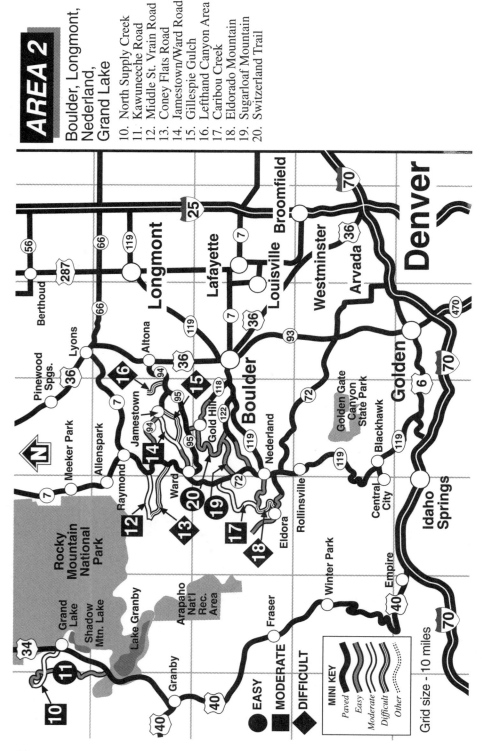

AREA 2

Boulder, Longmont,
Nederland,
Grand Lake

10. North Supply Creek
11. Kawuneeche Road
12. Middle St. Vrain Road
13. Coney Flats Road
14. Jamestown/Ward Road
15. Gillespie Gulch
16. Lefthand Canyon Area
17. Caribou Creek
18. Eldorado Mountain
19. Sugarloaf Mountain
20. Switzerland Trail

MINI KEY

Paved
Easy
Moderate
Difficult
Other

EASY

MODERATE

DIFFICULT

Grid size - 10 miles

Boulder, Longmont, Nederland, Grand Lake

You won't have to drive far between most of the trails in this area. Eight of the trails fit inside a ten mile circle and are within a short drive from Boulder and Longmont. Tucked away between ever-expanding residential areas are some of the most historic and beautiful backroads of Colorado. Many of the trails connect to the gorgeous Peak to Peak Highway, winding its way north from historic Blackhawk—now a big time gambling town—to picturesque Estes Park—gateway to Rocky Mountain National Park. On your way to the Switzerland Trail (Trail #20), a former railroad route, you'll pass through the still-active town of Gold Hill, where buildings remain much the same as they were 100 years ago. You'll be amazed that back-roads, so close to a major city, could have such a remote quality.

A little farther away, on the western side of Rocky Mountain National Park, are two trails that look down on three of Colorado's most popular lakes—Grand Lake, Shadow Mountain Lake, and Lake Granby. Take plenty of camera film; everywhere you look is a picture postcard setting.

The only thing missing from this store in historic Gold Hill is a place to tie your horse.

As you approach the top, the trail is more difficult than this picture appears.

Easy sections like this are rare. It's one of few places where you can see above the trees.

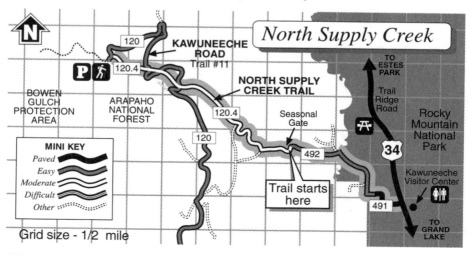

North Supply Creek

KAWUNEECHE ROAD
Trail #11

NORTH SUPPLY CREEK TRAIL

120

120.4

120.4

120

492

Seasonal Gate

Trail starts here

491

BOWEN GULCH PROTECTION AREA

ARAPAHO NATIONAL FOREST

TO ESTES PARK

Trail Ridge Road

Rocky Mountain National Park

34

Kawuneeche Visitor Center

TO GRAND LAKE

MINI KEY
Paved
Easy
Moderate
Difficult
Other

Grid size - 1/2 mile

North Supply Creek 10

Location: West of Grand Lake and Rocky Mountain National Park.

Difficulty: Moderate. This trail starts easy and gradually becomes more difficult as you climb. There are some rocky sections along the way. Careful tire placement and good driving skills are needed for stock, high-clearance vehicles. The nice thing about this trail is you can bail out at any time as it crisscrosses easier Kawuneeche Road (Trail #11) several times.

Features: Next to Rocky Mountain National Park, Grand Lake, and Shadow Mountain Lake. Provides a quick opportunity to escape the crowds. Once on the trail, views are limited by the trees.

Time & Distance: It is 4.3 miles from the Forest Service gate to the parking area at the end of the trail. Allow about 1 hour one way.

To Get There: From Denver, take Interstate 70 west and US 40 north. Just after the town of Granby, turn right and follow US 34 to the town of Grand Lake. Bear left at Grand Lake, following signs to Rocky Mountain National Park. In another 1.5 miles, turn left on paved County Rd. 491 just after the Kawuneeche Visitor Center. Follow this road 1.6 miles and turn left on F.S. 492. Go another 0.7 miles to the forest entrance marked with a gate.

An alternate route is to take Trail Ridge Road through Rocky Mountain National Park.

Trail Description: Reset your odometer at the starting point shown on the map. Bear right at 0.5 miles. Bear right again at 1.6, following signs for F.S 120.4. You begin to climb more aggressively with occasional views at several open areas. At 2.5 miles you'll cross over Kawuneeche Rd. 120 (Trail #11). Make a quick right and quick left. North Supply Creek Trail continues to be marked as F.S. 120.4. Bear left at a fork before you cross F.S. 120 again at 2.9 and 3.0 miles. At 4.2 miles, F.S. 120.4 ends at F.S. 120. Turn left to reach a parking area and hiking trail at 4.3 miles.

Return Trip: Return the way you came or via Kawuneeche Rd. (Trail #11).

Services: Restrooms at the Kawauneeche Visitor Center, gas in Grand Lake.

Maps: Trails Illustrated Rocky Mountain National Park #200, Arapaho National Forest, Colorado Atlas and Gazetteer.

View of Lake Granby from US 34, very near the start of the Kawuneeche Road.

This road is beautiful in the fall.

Looking down on Shadow Mountain Lake.

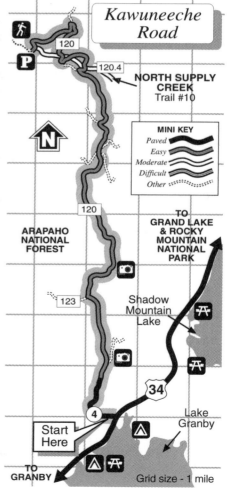

Kawuneeche Road

120
120.4

NORTH SUPPLY CREEK
Trail #10

N

MINI KEY
Paved
Easy
Moderate
Difficult
Other

120

ARAPAHO NATIONAL FOREST

123

TO GRAND LAKE & ROCKY MOUNTAIN NATIONAL PARK

Shadow Mountain Lake

34

Lake Granby

Start Here

4

TO GRANBY

Grid size - 1 mile

Kawuneeche Road 11

Location: West of Rocky Mountain National Park and Grand Lake.

Difficulty: Easy. A smooth, wide gravel road all the way to the top.

Features: An enjoyable scenic drive which looks down on Grand Lake, Shadow Mountain Lake, and Lake Granby. Near the Kawuneeche Visitor Center.

Time & Distance: The trail is about 12 miles. Allow about 1 hour each way.

To Get There: From Denver, take Interstate 70 west and US 40 north. Just after the town of Granby, turn right and follow US 34 to the north side of Lake Granby. Watch for County Road 4 on the left just after some storage buildings and across from the Dilly Dock Marina. You can also reach Kawuneeche Road by traveling through Rocky Mountain National Park and heading south on Trail Ridge Road.

Trail Description: Reset your odometer when you turn off US 34. The first couple of miles are paved and route-finding is easy. At 3 miles bear right following signs for F.S. 120. Bear left at 7 miles, as lesser South Supply Creek Trail goes right. Smaller spur roads will begin branching off. Stay on the main road. At 9.1 miles, North Supply Creek (Trail #10) enters on the right. You will cross it several more times. Bear left at 10.9 and 11.9 miles. The road ends at a parking area at 12.3 miles.

Return Trip: Return the way you came or exit on the more difficult North Supply Creek Trail. It brings you out near the Kawuneeche Visitor Center.

Services: Full services in the town of Grand Lake, which is several miles north of the start of the Kawuneeche Road on US 34.

Other Activities: Hiking, horseback riding, mountain biking, ATVs and snowmobiles are permitted beyond the parking area. You can hike all the way to the Never Summer Wilderness. Stop at the Kawuneeche Visitor Center north of Grand Lake. Boat, fish, and camp at the lakes. Visit Rocky Mountain National Park just a few miles north on US 34.

Maps: Trails Illustrated Rocky Mountain National Park #200, Arapaho National Forest, Colorado Atlas and Gazetteer.

The start of the trail is well marked.

One of several challenging rocky sections.

Timberline Falls, a short hike from the road.

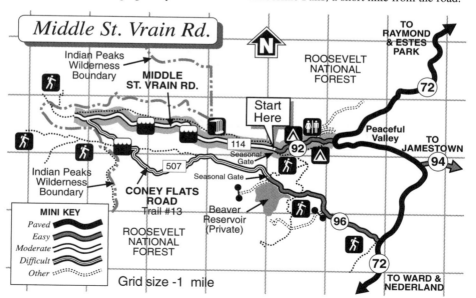

Middle St. Vrain Rd.

N

Indian Peaks Wilderness Boundary

MIDDLE ST. VRAIN RD.

ROOSEVELT NATIONAL FOREST

TO RAYMOND & ESTES PARK

72

Start Here

Peaceful Valley

114

92

TO JAMESTOWN

94

507

Seasonal Gate

Seasonal Gate

Indian Peaks Wilderness Boundary

CONEY FLATS ROAD
Trail #13

Beaver Reservoir (Private)

96

72

MINI KEY
Paved
Easy
Moderate
Difficult
Other

ROOSEVELT NATIONAL FOREST

TO WARD & NEDERLAND

Grid size - 1 mile

Middle St. Vrain Road 12

Location: Northwest of Boulder. South of Estes Park.

Difficulty: Moderate. This trail is not steep, however, there are a few challenging rough spots which require high ground clearance and careful tire placement. Skid plates are recommended.

Features: You pass by two popular Forest Service campgrounds on the way to the start of the trail. Camping is allowed along the trail after 0.7 miles. Numerous hiking and cross country ski trails in the area connect to a large network of trails into the Indian Peaks Wilderness. Follow signs on a short hike to the Timberline Falls. (See photo.) Hike to the St. Vrain Glacier, Rocky Mountain National Park, and the Arapaho National Recreation Area on the west side of the Continental Divide.

Time & Distance: Less than 4 miles one way. It can be driven in less than 1 hour one way, however, allow extra time for sight seeing.

To Get There: From Boulder, take Boulder Canyon Road 119 west to Nederland. Go north on Route 72 to Peaceful Valley. Follow signs to the Camp Dick and Peaceful Valley F.S. Campgrounds on the left. After leaving Route 72, it is 1.1 miles to the start of the trail. You'll pass both of the above campgrounds. You can also reach this trail from Estes Park. Head south on Route 7 and southwest on Route 72.

Trail Description: Reset your odometer at the start. At 1.0 miles, you'll cross the first of several logs embedded in the ground. Cross on an angle to avoid getting high centered. After several small stream crossings and rocky sections, you reach the turn for Coney Flats Road F.S. 507 (Trail #13) on the left. Middle St. Vrain soon dead ends at the Indian Peaks Wilderness.

Return Trip: Return the way you came or via the difficult Coney Flats Road (Trail #13).

Services: Full services in Nederland and Estes Park. There are modern pit toilets at the campgrounds.

Maps: Trails Illustrated Indian Peaks, Gold Hill #102, Arapaho National Forest, Colorado Atlas and Gazetteer.

This deep crossing at Coney Creek is the most challenging spot of the trail. Use caution.

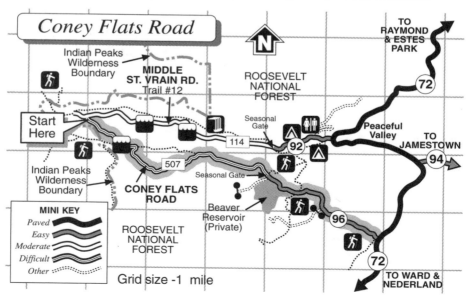

Luckily, my camera was ready when I came upon this large elk by the side of the road.

Coney Flats Road

TO RAYMOND & ESTES PARK

Indian Peaks Wilderness Boundary

MIDDLE ST. VRAIN RD. Trail #12

ROOSEVELT NATIONAL FOREST

N

72

Start Here

Seasonal Gate

114

Peaceful Valley

TO JAMESTOWN

92

94

Indian Peaks Wilderness Boundary

507

CONEY FLATS ROAD

Seasonal Gate

Beaver Reservoir (Private)

96

MINI KEY

Paved
Easy
Moderate
Difficult
Other

ROOSEVELT NATIONAL FOREST

Grid size -1 mile

72

TO WARD & NEDERLAND

Coney Flats Road ◆13◆

Location: Northwest of Boulder. South of Estes Park.

Difficulty: Difficult. The first part of the trail, between Middle St. Vrain Road (Trail #12) and Coney Creek is rocky, narrow, and steep. The crossing at Coney Creek is deep. When I went through in September, the water came to the top of my 32 inch tires. It would be deeper in the spring. After the creek, the trail becomes progressively easier.

Features: There are numerous hiking and cross-country ski trails in the area which connect to a large network of trails into the Indian Peaks Wilderness. Beaver Reservoir is privately owned.

Time & Distance: Coney Flats Road is 4.8 miles from its start to Beaver Reservoir and another 2.6 to Highway 72. Allow 1 to 2 hours one way. Remember to allow about an hour to drive Middle St. Vrain Road first.

To Get There: Follow directions to Middle St. Vrain Road (Trail #12). From the start of Middle St. Vrain Road, drive 3.6 miles west. Coney Flats Road F.S. 507 goes up the hill sharply to the left.

Trail Description: Reset your odometer at the start. The trail begins to climb immediately through the trees. Although rocky and narrow, well-equipped vehicles will have little difficulty. Lockers are helpful but not required. You reach a gate and a clearing at 0.7 miles followed by the Coney Creek water crossing shown on the opposite page. I watched some-one else drive through first so I could see the depth of the water. It may be too deep to cross in the spring. At 1.3 miles bear right as a hiking trail goes straight. Bear right again at 1.6 miles. At 3.2 miles the hiking trail rejoins the road. Bear left at 3.8 miles. The trail ends at 4.8 miles at Beaver Reservoir and joins County Road 96. Turn left to get back to Highway 72.

Return Trip: At Highway 72, left leads to Raymond, Lyons, or Estes Park. Right takes you to Ward, Nederland, and eventually to Boulder.

Services: Full services in Nederland and Estes Park. There are modern pit toilets at the campgrounds on Middle St. Vrain Road.

Maps: Trails Illustrated Indian Peaks, Gold Hill #102, Arapaho National Forest, Colorado Atlas and Gazetteer.

Departing from Jamestown.

The upper portion of the trail is easy.

James Creek crossing is wide but shallow.

This spot is steep and slippery if wet.

Jamestown / Ward Road 14

Location: Northwest of Boulder between Jamestown and Ward.

Difficulty: Moderate. This rating is based on dry conditions. If wet, the trail is difficult. There is one long steep hill with a dirt surface that becomes slippery after a period of rain. Several rocky sections require careful tire placement. High ground clearance and skid plates are recommended.

Features: The eastern half of this trail climbs steeply over rough terrain through an area that is infrequently used. It is an out-of-the-way area that I would not recommend for family outings. The western half is easy and passes through a beautiful private resort and you must stay on the road as you pass through. Please drive slowly and quietly. You'll pass picturesque Gold Lake. If you take photos, do it quickly from the road and move on. Hard-core four-wheelers do not have to pass through the resort. They can return to Jamestown via difficult Gillespie Gulch (Trail #15).

Time & Distance: It's about 8 miles from Jamestown to Highway 72 near Ward. The easy portion of the trail is about half the distance. Allow 1 to 2 hours one way.

To Get There: From Boulder, take US 36 north to Altona. Turn west on Lefthand Canyon Road marked as County Rd. 94. Follow 94 all the way to Jamestown. In Jamestown, turn left on Ward Street. It is the last street on the left as you pass through town.

To start at the other end of the trail, follow Lefthand Canyon Road 95 to Ward. Head north 0.3 miles on Highway 72. Turn right on a dirt road across from the Millsite Bar and follow signs to Gold Lake.

Trail Description: Reset your odometer when you turn off County Rd. 94 at Jamestown. You'll pass through an older residential area as the road quickly gets rough. The road parallels rugged James Creek on the left. Next to the stream, portions of the trail are quite photogenic. At 2.2 miles, bear left at an unmarked fork. To the right is a meadow with possible camping spots. At 2.8 miles, you pass a mine on the right that looks more like a junkyard. At 3.1 miles, you'll cross over James Creek as pictured on the opposite page. The crossing is wide but fairly shallow. Use caution in the spring or after a heavy rain. At 3.4 miles, another unmarked road goes to the left. You should continue straight as the road starts climbing rather steeply. This part of the road is dirt with some significant undulations. It could be very difficult to climb if wet. As the road levels out, you'll come to F.S. 509 on the left at about 4.0 miles. This road takes you back down to Jamestown through difficult Gillespie Gulch (Trail #15).

To reach Ward, continue on what becomes an easy road. Bear right at subsequent forks until you reach Gold Lake. At 4.9 miles pass through a gate at a private resort. Gold Lake is on the left. With its background of white capped mountains on the horizon, it is a striking sight. The road becomes smooth gravel. Drive slowly and stay on the road at all times. Turn left at 7.8 miles before reaching paved Highway 72 at 8.1 miles.

Return Trip: Turn left on Highway 72 back to Lefthand Canyon Road County Rd. 95 in about 0.3 miles. If you turn left on Lefthand Canyon Road it will take you through Ward then downhill back to Boulder. If you continue on Highway 72 south, you will reach Nederland. At Nederland, head east on Highway 119 through scenic Boulder Canyon and eventually back to Boulder.

Services: Full services in Boulder and Nederland. Ward had a small general store.

Other Activities: You can hike, mountain bike, and horseback ride on the upper scenic parts of the trail, however, there are no separate designated trails for such activities. Everyone shares the road with various types of vehicles. This is why it is important to drive slowly. Be courteous to hikers and bikers. Drive extremely slow around horses. When appropriate, pull over and shut off your engine and let them go by you.

Just north of Ward on Highway 72, there is a paved road that heads west to the Brainard Lake Recreation Area. This is a pleasant drive that offers the best view of the Indian Peaks Wilderness. Forest Service activities include hiking, fishing, camping, and cross-country skiing in the winter. Many of the hiking trails are easy and suitable for children.

Historical Highlights: Take a few minutes to visit Ward. Try to imagine the place over 100 years ago as a vibrant and prosperous mining town. After being destroyed by fire in 1900, it was rebuilt. By 1904, it grew to become the largest town in Boulder County with its own newspaper, railroad depot, and an excellent school. Today the school is used for the town hall, post office, and library. The original Congregational Church still stands and is listed in the National Register of Historic Places.

Maps: Trails Illustrated Indian Peaks, Gold Hill #102, Roosevelt National Forest, Colorado Atlas and Gazetteer.

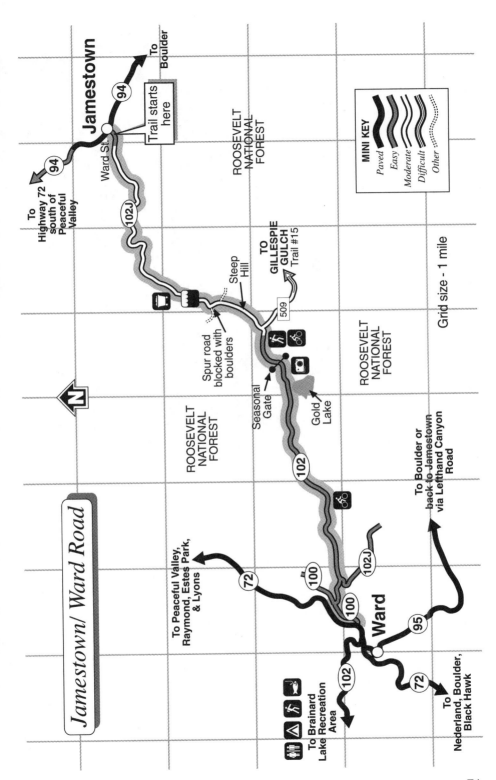

Jamestown/ Ward Road

Jamestown

94 — To Boulder

94 — To Highway 72 south of Peaceful Valley

Trail starts here

Ward St.

102J

ROOSEVELT NATIONAL FOREST

Steep Hill

Spur road blocked with boulders

TO GILLESPIE GULCH
Trail #15

509

Seasonal Gate

Gold Lake

102

ROOSEVELT NATIONAL FOREST

ROOSEVELT NATIONAL FOREST

N

72 — To Peaceful Valley, Raymond, Estes Park, & Lyons

100

102J

100

Ward

95 — To Boulder or back to Jamestown via Lefthand Canyon Road

72 — To Nederland, Boulder, Black Hawk

102 — To Brainard Lake Recreation Area

MINI KEY
Paved
Easy
Moderate
Difficult
Other

Grid size - 1 mile

71

This photo barely captures steepness of hill.

The beginning of the trail is easy.

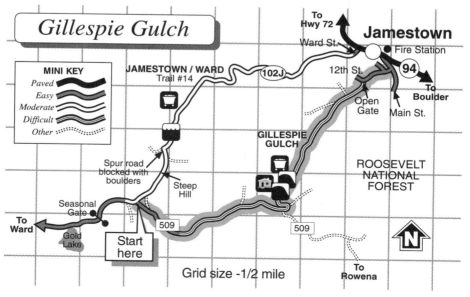

You pass this well-preserved old miners cabin near one of the obstacles.

Gillespie Gulch

MINI KEY
Paved
Easy
Moderate
Difficult
Other

JAMESTOWN / WARD
Trail #14

102J

To
Hwy 72

Jamestown

Ward St.

Fire Station

12th St.

94

To
Boulder

Open
Gate

Main St.

GILLESPIE GULCH

ROOSEVELT NATIONAL FOREST

Spur road blocked with boulders

Steep Hill

Seasonal Gate

To Ward

Gold Lake

Start here

509

509

To
Rowena

N

Grid size -1/2 mile

Gillespie Gulch ◆15▶

Location: Northwest of Boulder. Southwest of Jamestown.

Difficulty: Difficult. Very steep inclines with large rocks in loose soil. Lockers and large tires are recommended.

Features: A challenging trail for the hard-core four-wheeler. Not extremely long, but several difficult spur roads can be explored to enhance the trip. Explore only authorized side roads. Obey all signs and barricades.

Time & Distance: From the start of the trail to Jamestown is about 4.5 miles. Depending upon conditions, it takes about 1 hour. Add additional time to drive up Jamestown/Ward Road (Trail #14).

To Get There: First, drive the eastern half of Jamestown/ Ward Road (Trail #14). It forms a loop as you return downhill through Gillespie Gulch. Avoid early temptations to explore spur roads until after you've completed this loop. See directions to Jamestown/Ward Road. Follow this road about 4 miles and turn left on F.S 509.

Trail Description: Reset your odometer at the start of F.S. 509. The road is easy at first as it traverses a fairly level area. Bear right at 1.4 miles as you start downhill on rougher terrain. At 1.9 miles, 509 goes to the right; you bear left. Immediately bear left again as you descend rapidly. The first tough spot is at 2.1 miles. At 2.2 miles, note cabin on the left. (See photo on opposite page.) At the cabin, you have a choice of two tough spots to the right. At 3.5 miles, bear right downhill as another road joins on the left. Bear right again at 3.7 miles. After a gate at 3.9 miles, turn right on 12th Street. When you reach Main Street at 4.3 miles, turn left. This takes you back to County Rd. 94 by the volunteer fire station in Jamestown.

Return Trip: At County Rd. 94, turn right to get back to US 36. From there, turn right for Boulder and left for Lyons and Longmont.

Services: Some services are found in Jamestown, otherwise return to Boulder.

Maps: Trails Illustrated Indian Peaks, Gold Hill #102, Roosevelt National Forest, Colorado Atlas and Gazetteer.

The *Squeeze* pushes you off-camber against this tree. Body damage is possible for hard tops.

This confusing intersection is called *Five Points*. Bear right uphill for the main trail.

Big Mother Hill begins straight ahead.

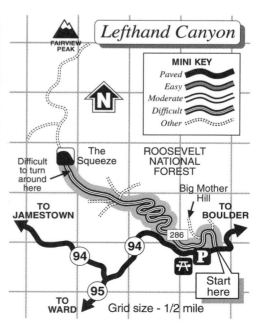

Lefthand Canyon

FAIRVIEW PEAK

MINI KEY
Paved
Easy
Moderate
Difficult
Other

N

Difficult to turn around here

The Squeeze

ROOSEVELT NATIONAL FOREST

Big Mother Hill

TO JAMESTOWN

TO BOULDER

286

94

94

95

TO WARD

Start here

Grid size - 1/2 mile

Lefthand Canyon Area ◀16▶

Location: Northwest of Boulder.

Difficulty: Difficult. Many steep, off-camber, and dangerous hillsides. Do not drive this trail alone or leave your vehicle unattended.

Features: A large network of trails. Route-finding is difficult but not *that* important since most people have no particular destination. Stay on existing trails at all times. If you can't decide whether a trail is legitimate, stay off.

Time & Distance: The trail as described here is about 2.4 miles and takes less than 1 hour each way. You can spend many hours exploring spur roads.

To Get There: From Boulder, take US 36 north to Altona. Turn west on Lefthand Canyon Road marked as County Rd. 94. Drive 3.7 miles west and turn right on F.S. 286 just before a sign for the Roosevelt National Forest.

Trail Description: The main trail described here takes you through the heart of this area and provides a reference point for many other trails. This trail has no particular significance, other than it eventually reaches the highest point in the area called Fairview Peak. You must turn around at the top.

Reset your odometer when you turn off the pavement. Turn left up a switchback at 0.2 miles. Bear left at 0.4 to stay on the main road. (Straight will take you up a series of difficult switchbacks called *Big Mother Hill).* The main road parallels a power line for a distance before reaching a confusing spot at 0.9 miles. Try to stay on the main road as it climbs the hill in a series of large sweeping switchbacks. If all goes well, at 1.4 miles you'll cross an off-camber rocky section before coming to *Five Points*, a complex intersection at 1.6 miles. Of the two roads that go uphill, take the one to the right (see photo at left). It gets very rocky before you encounter the *Squeeze* at 2.4 miles. This obstacle tilts you against a nasty tree (see photo). Because of my hard top and long wheel base, I elected to turn back here. Fairview Peak is another 2.5 miles over very difficult and confusing terrain. Proceed at your own risk.

Return Trip: Return the way you came.

Services: Nothing in the area. Return to Boulder.

Maps: Roosevelt National Forest, Colorado Atlas and Gazetteer.

Early sun warms a crisp morning.

This section can get muddy after a rain.

Caribou Creek was fairly shallow when this photo was taken in late September.

An open meadow with a view of Indian Peaks Wilderness in the distance.

Caribou Creek 17

Location: West of Nederland near the Indian Peaks Wilderness.

Difficulty: Moderate. With the exception of a couple of miles, most of this trail is an easy gravel road. The moderate portion can become quite muddy during the spring and after heavy rains. During this time, difficult conditions are possible. The low portion of the trail near the creek may be closed when the trail is too wet.

Features: Getting to this trail is an easy and beautiful drive from Boulder to Nederland—an interesting and bustling little mountain town. The trail connects to Rainbow Lakes F.S. Campground immediately adjacent to the Indian Peaks Wilderness. You'll pass through the historic townsite of Caribou, described later.

Time & Distance: The total length of this backroad from the time you leave Highway 72 until you return to 72 is 11.4 miles. Add another 2 miles for the side trip to Rainbow Lakes Campground. Allow 2 to 3 hours.

To Get There: From the center of Boulder, travel west on Canyon Boulevard, which becomes Boulder Canyon Road 119 once you leave town. When you reach the roundabout in Nederland, follow Highway 72 north about 7 miles. Turn left at signs to the University of Colorado Camp which is on County Road 116, also marked as F.S. 298.

Trail Description: Reset your odometer as you turn off Highway 72 onto 116, an easy gravel road. Bear left at one mile. At 3.4 miles, bear left again at a small bridge over North Boulder Creek. You'll come to a fork at 4.3 miles. Left takes you to Caribou; right takes you to Rainbow Lakes F.S. Campground. Even if you have no plans to camp now, take a few extra minutes to look at the campground. It adds only 2 miles total to the trip. There are two hiking trails at the campground which are described in "Other Activities" on the next page. When you return to this fork after visiting the campground, your odometer should read 6.3 miles. Turn right, following a sign for Caribou Road F.S. 505.

From this point, camping along the road is prohibited and subject to a $1,000 fine! In addition, you must stay on F.S. 505 at all times. Past abuses by irresponsible drivers have damaged the surrounding area, forcing the Forest Service to block many side roads. At 6.6 miles, bear right. After that you'll descend an undulating hill. Conditions may vary depending upon recency of maintenance. Cross Caribou Creek at 6.9 miles. It is fairly shallow most of the time, but inspect it yourself to be sure. As soon as you cross the creek, bear right; the left is blocked. The next little stretch can get muddy. Consider the possibility of getting stuck before you proceed. After this section, you cross a meadow and head back into the trees at 7.3 miles where the trail becomes somewhat rocky and narrow. Bear left at 8.8 miles. There's a gate at 9.1 miles and another at 9.2 miles.

After you pass through the second gate, there is a wide area to park. This is the townsite of Caribou. There is nothing left of Caribou, the town, except remnants of a couple of stone structures farther down the hill. (See Historical Highlights.) A hard right here takes you to the town of Eldora on difficult Eldorado Mountain Trail #18. To reach Nederland, turn left and head downhill on easy Caribou Road County Rd. 128. Bear right at 12.0 miles before reaching Highway 72 at 13.4 miles. Nederland is to the right.

Return Trip: From Nederland, circle the roundabout and head back down Boulder Canyon Road 119 to Boulder.

Services: Full services in Nederland. There are pit toilets at the Rainbow Lakes Campground.

Other Activities: Stop in at the Nederland Visitor Center as it is just around the corner south of the roundabout. There you will find some helpful folks and interesting historical information. The more you know about the area, the more you will enjoy your trip. If you stop at the Rainbow Lakes Campground, you can hike into the Indian Peaks Wilderness. The hike to Rainbow Lakes is short. The Indian Peaks hike is for serious backpackers. It heads over the Continental Divide to the Arapaho Glaciers.

Historical Highlights: Colorado's first major silver rush took place in what is now the barren valley at the end of Caribou Road. As you pass through the last Forest Service gate, try to imagine what life was like here in the 1870s. Miners from all over the world flocked to this place after a rich silver deposit was discovered in 1869. Development of the town was rapid. Before long there were houses, stores, hotels, dance halls, blacksmith shops, numerous businesses and a weekly newspaper. It is estimated that $8 million was extracted from these hills in little more than a decade. Most of the mines were located on the hillside east of the intersection of F.S. 505 and Caribou Road. You can hike to a cemetery in the same location.

Maps: Trails Illustrated Indian Peaks, Gold Hill #102, Roosevelt National Forest, Colorado Atlas and Gazetteer.

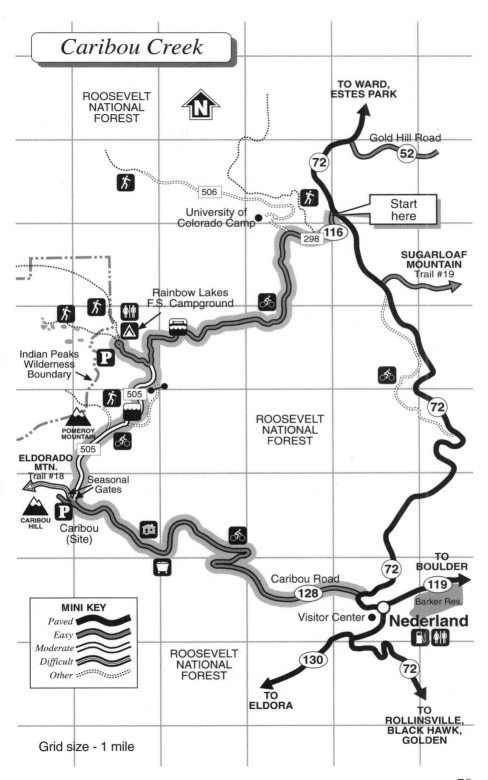

Caribou Creek

ROOSEVELT
NATIONAL
FOREST

N

**TO WARD,
ESTES PARK**

Gold Hill Road
72 · 52

506

University of
Colorado Camp

298 · 116

Start
here

**SUGARLOAF
MOUNTAIN**
Trail #19

Rainbow Lakes
F.S. Campground

Indian Peaks
Wilderness
Boundary

P

505

**POMEROY
MOUNTAIN**

505

**ELDORADO
MTN.**
Trail #18

Seasonal
Gates

**CARIBOU
HILL**

P

Caribou
(Site)

**ROOSEVELT
NATIONAL
FOREST**

72

**TO
BOULDER**

72

119

Barker Res.

Caribou Road
128

Visitor Center

Nederland

MINI KEY
Paved
Easy
Moderate
Difficult
Other

**ROOSEVELT
NATIONAL
FOREST**

130

**TO
ELDORA**

72

**TO
ROLLINSVILLE,
BLACK HAWK,
GOLDEN**

Grid size - 1 mile

This is the toughest spot on the trail. It is not encountered until the last part of the trip.

Looking across the valley at the Eldora Ski Area. Notice a dusting of snow in early October.

Eldorado Mountain ◀18▶

Location: West of Boulder and Nederland. North of Eldora.

Difficulty: Difficult. Most of the trail is easy-to-moderate except for a difficult spot at the top and another at the bottom. The bottom of the trail is very narrow and off-camber. Branches will brush against your vehicle. Wide vehicles will find it difficult to turn on the switchbacks. Long wheel-based vehicles are not recommended.

Features: The trail is not extremely long but several spur roads can be explored to extend the trip. Eldora Ski Area and the Indian Peaks Wilderness provide pleasing views. The lower portion of the trail is challenging and fun.

Time & Distance: The trail is less than 6 miles. Allow 1 to 2 hours depending upon the capability and width of your vehicle. Wide vehicles will take more time to get through the lower part.

To Get There: From Boulder, take Boulder Canyon Road 119 west to Nederland. At the roundabout in Nederland, bear right and follow Highway 72 just 0.4 miles north. Turn left on well-marked Caribou Road. Drive 4.3 miles and bear right uphill. Caribou Road ends in another 1.1 miles at a wide parking area. There are two large Forest Service gates on the right. A sharp right leads to Caribou Creek Trail #17. Slightly right is Eldorado Mountain, marked as F.S. 505D. The road may be closed if conditions are too wet. Check with the Forest Service if you have any doubts.

Trail Description: Reset your odometer at the start. At 0.3 miles, bear left uphill into the trees. Bear left again at 0.7 miles at a fork marked 505A. You begin to climb uphill over a fairly tough rocky section. When I drove through this section in early October, the trail was snow-covered and challenging. At 1.0 miles, bear left again at an unmarked fork. Bear right at 1.1 as it begins to flatten out and becomes easier. At 1.3 miles 505A intersects with 505. Bear right. This trail previously intersected this point from Caribou Road around the southeast side of Caribou Hill, but is now blocked. Bear left at 1.5 and right at 1.7 at unmarked intersections. Bear right again at 2.3 miles as you begin to go downhill into the trees.

   The next stretch is uneventful as you cross a variety of moderate terrain. At 4.6 miles you begin to see more of the valley below as the terrain gets steeper and narrower. A tight switchback follows a rocky off-camber section at 4.7 miles. The trail becomes a narrow shelf road before reaching the toughest obstacle at 5.0 miles. It is rocky, narrow, and off-camber (see photo). I stacked a few rocks so my left front tire wouldn't drop down too far. The trail continues to be rocky and narrow until you reach a seasonal closure gate at 5.7 miles. Please be quiet and courteous as you pass several residences. Two quick left turns put you on Huron Avenue. At 5.9 miles, turn left as Huron Avenue intersects with paved road 130.

Return Trip: *Reset your odometer as you turn left on County Road 130.* At 1.8 miles the road from Eldora Ski Area joins 130 on the right. Highway 72 is reached at 3.1 miles. The roundabout at Nederland is 0.5 miles to the left where 119 takes you back to Boulder. Right at 72 takes you to Rollinsville, Black Hawk, and Golden.

Services: Full services in Nederland.

Other Activities: A right turn at County Rd. 130 will take you through the residential community of Eldora. Many buildings here are listed in the National Register of Historic Places. Several hiking and cross-country ski trails are located in this area. Continuing west, on what becomes Hessie Road, takes you to the Buckingham F.S. Campground with additional hiking and cross-country ski trails. Stop in at the Nederland Visitor Center for detailed information on all the activities in the area.

Historical Highlights: Both Nederland and Eldora have interesting mining histories. Nederland, because of its location between Black Hawk, Central City, and Boulder, became an important freighting and milling center during the mining years. It experienced three separate periods of boom and bust, once for gold, once for silver, and finally for tungsten. It presently is a thriving tourist supported community.

Eldora experienced its glory years in the late 1890s with the mining of gold on nearby Spencer Mountain. The town soon grew to over one thousand people, but because the gold was difficult to extract from the ore, profits never materialized to the expected degree. Eldora, like so many other Colorado towns, now counts on tourism and skiing to help pay its bills.

Maps: Trails Illustrated Indian Peaks, Gold Hill #102, Roosevelt National Forest, Colorado Atlas and Gazetteer.

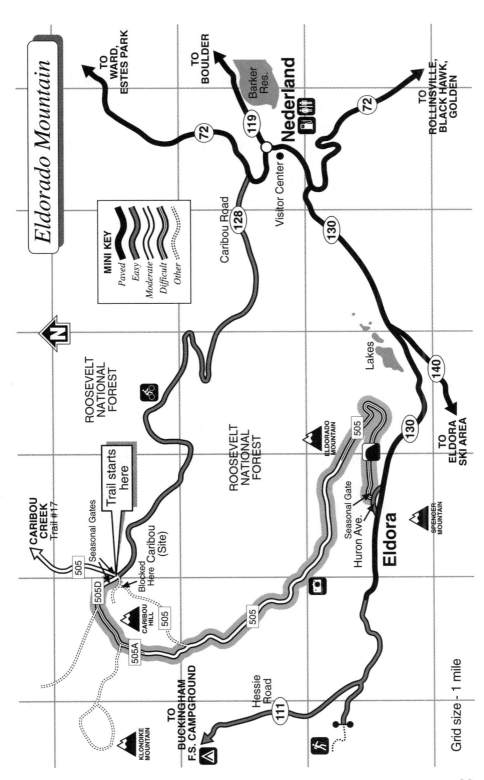

Eldorado Mountain

TO WARD, ESTES PARK

TO BOULDER

Nederland

Barker Res.

Visitor Center

72

119

128

130

72

TO ROLLINSVILLE, BLACK HAWK, GOLDEN

Caribou Road

MINI KEY
Paved
Easy
Moderate
Difficult
Other

N

ROOSEVELT NATIONAL FOREST

ROOSEVELT NATIONAL FOREST

Lakes

140

130

TO ELDORA SKI AREA

ELDORADO MOUNTAIN

505

Trail starts here

CARIBOU CREEK Trail #17

Seasonal Gates

505

505D

Blocked Here Caribou (Site)

CARIBOU HILL

505

505A

Seasonal Gate

Huron Ave.

SPENCER MOUNTAIN

Eldora

505

KLONDIKE MOUNTAIN

TO BUCKINGHAM F.S. CAMPGROUND

Hessie Road

111

Grid size - 1 mile

83

Although the road is easy, you should still go slow and use caution around blind curves.

The western side of the road is more open with beautiful vistas at several points.

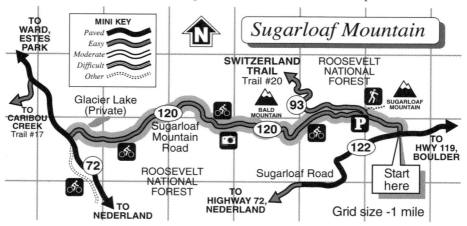

TO WARD, ESTES PARK

MINI KEY
Paved
Easy
Moderate
Difficult
Other

N

Sugarloaf Mountain

SWITZERLAND TRAIL
Trail #20

ROOSEVELT NATIONAL FOREST

BALD MOUNTAIN

93

SUGARLOAF MOUNTAIN

TO CARIBOU CREEK
Trail #17

Glacier Lake (Private)

120

Sugarloaf Mountain Road

120

P

TO HWY 119, BOULDER

72

ROOSEVELT NATIONAL FOREST

122

Sugarloaf Road

Start here

TO NEDERLAND

TO HIGHWAY 72, NEDERLAND

Grid size -1 mile

Sugarloaf Mountain 19

Location: West of Boulder.

Difficulty: Easy. A mildly rocky road suitable for any stock sport utility vehicle under dry conditions. Route-finding is easy.

Features: A short, beautiful, relaxing drive close to Boulder. The road follows the course of an old railroad bed. A popular trail to view the changing color of the aspens in the fall.

Time & Distance: A little more than 6 miles from the pavement of Sugarloaf Road 122 to Highway 72. Allow about 1 hour plus stops.

To Get There: From the center of Boulder, travel west on Canyon Boulevard which becomes Boulder Canyon Road 119 once you leave town. After about 5 miles, watch for signs to Sugarloaf Road 122 on the right. Follow this paved road 4.7 miles to Sugarloaf Mountain Road 120 on the right.

Trail Description: Reset your odometer when you turn off paved road 122. Follow Sugarloaf Mountain Road up the hill through a residential area 0.8 miles to a wide parking area. Take the road to the left. From here the road is fairly flat and views are marvelous. Several spur roads join Sugarloaf Mountain Road along the way but the main road is obvious. Bear left at 3.2 miles. At 5.1 miles, you leave the Roosevelt National Forest and pass through private property. Please respect the rights of the property owners. Paved Highway 72 is reached at 6.2 miles.

Return Trip: To get back to Boulder, turn left on 72 to Nederland. From there take 119 east. Turning right on 72 will take you to Ward and Estes Park.

Services: Full services in Nederland and Boulder.

Other Activities: Hike to the top of Sugarloaf Mountain from a hiking trail that departs at the east side of the parking area. Many people park here and mountain bike west on Sugarloaf Mountain Road. It is flat and easy.

Maps: Trails Illustrated Indian Peaks, Gold Hill #102, Roosevelt National Forest, Colorado Atlas and Gazetteer.

Because the trail follows the original railroad grade, the angle of descent is gradual.

The town of Sunset. Directions will bring you down upper right road and depart lower left.

SUVs have no trouble driving through these cuts, built wide enough for trains.

Switzerland Trail ⑳

Location: West of Boulder.

Difficulty: Easy. Gentle grades provide a relaxing drive. The trail narrows to one lane in places so use caution around blind curves. The road surface is mildly rocky and suitable, under dry conditions, for any stock sport utility vehicle.

Features: Follows the old railroad bed of the Switzerland Trail Railway. Views are spectacular along the entire length of the trail. On the way to the starting point, you pass through the historic town of Gold Hill where some buildings, like the Gold Hill Store, remain much the same as they were over 100 years ago. (See Historical Highlights on the next page.)

Time & Distance: The trail is 8.6 miles long from Gold Hill Road to the parking area at Sugarloaf Mountain. Allow 1 to 2 hours driving time. Consider driving Sugarloaf Mountain (Trail #19) after you complete the Switzerland Trail. It ends at the parking area where Sugarloaf Mountain starts and is a natural continuation point.

To Get There: From the center of Boulder, travel west on Canyon Boulevard which becomes Boulder Canyon Road 119 once you leave town. A few miles west of town, turn right on Fourmile Canyon Road 118. In another 4.8 miles, Fourmile Canyon Road 118 goes left to the town of Sunset. You go right on Road 89. Gold Hill is 3.9 miles farther. Turn left at Main Street in Gold Hill. After 0.3 miles through town, go straight. This puts you on Gold Hill Road 52. Watch for a large sign for the Switzerland Trail on the left in another 2.6 miles. The sign also indicates Mont Alto Picnic Grounds and Sunset Townsite is in this direction. This is the start of the trail.

Trail Description: Reset your odometer at the start and head south. At 1.1 miles, you pass the Mont Alto Picnic Grounds. In 1898, there was a popular daytime resort here used by guests of the railroad. A lone chimney is all that remains of a large pavilion. From here, the trail winds down the mountainside to the townsite of Sunset at 4.6 miles. Several residences are located at the townsite. Be courteous as you pass through. To end the trip here, turn left down Fourmile Canyon Road back to Highway 119.

    To continue on the Switzerland Trail, go straight through Sunset. Bear right then left immediately. At 4.7 miles bear left as Pennsylvania Gulch goes to the right. Continue to bear left as two spur roads go right at 5.5 and 5.8 miles. At 7.3 there is an overlook to the left. The scenery improves before reaching a wide parking area at 8.6 miles, just below the Summit of Sugarloaf Mountain. Turn left here to end the trip. Right takes you west on Sugarloaf Mountain Road (Trail #19).

Return Trip: To end the trip, turn left at the large parking area and head downhill 0.8 miles through a residential area. Turn left on paved road 122 and go 4.7 miles to Highway 119. Left takes you to Boulder.

Services: Gold Hill has a few small, interesting stores. You'll have to return to Boulder for full services.

Other Activities: All of the roads in this area are very popular for hiking, mountain biking, and cross-country skiing in the winter.

Historical Highlights: In 1858, Gold Hill became the first permanent mining settlement in what was then part of the Nebraska Territory. (Colorado did not become a state until 1876.) The first settlement was short-lived because mining techniques at that time did not allow for economical extraction of gold from the ore. A second gold rush occurred in 1872 after new techniques of gold removal were developed. In 1873, the Wentworth Hotel was built. A porch and dormers were added in 1921 and the hotel still stands today as the Blue Bird Lodge. A dining area was added in 1926 and today it is recognized as the well known Gold Hill Inn Restaurant.

The first railroad in the area didn't arrive until 1883. It came up from Boulder through Fourmile Canyon to the town of Sunset. Fifteen years later, a northern extension was added to the town of Ward. This is the first part of the trip described here. The railroad would stop at the Mont Alto Pavilion, now just a picnic area. Later in 1905, the southern route was added to reach the new mining town of Eldora. This is the part of the road that goes from Sunset to the parking area at Sugarloaf Mountain. Sugarloaf Mountain Road (Trail #19) follows the old railroad bed that eventually reached Eldora. As the automobile and trucking came of age, the railroad declined. In 1919, a flood washed out much of the track and several bridges bringing to an end a glorious era in Boulder County. The remaining track was removed and sold to other railroads. One of the engines from this railroad is now on display in Boulder's Central Park.

Maps: Trails Illustrated Indian Peaks, Gold Hill #102, Roosevelt National Forest, Colorado Atlas and Gazetteer.

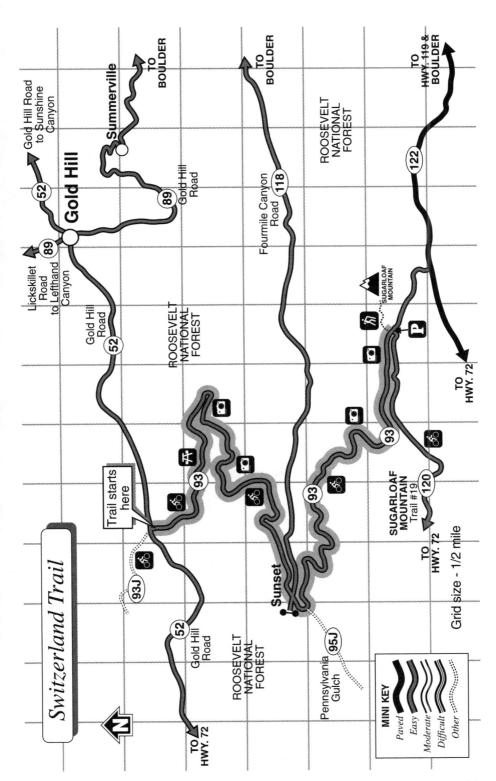

Switzerland Trail

N

TO HWY. 72

Gold Hill Road

52

ROOSEVELT NATIONAL FOREST

93J

Trail starts here

93

Sunset

93

95J

Pennsylvania Gulch

93

120

TO HWY. 72

SUGARLOAF MOUNTAIN Trail #19

SUGARLOAF MOUNTAIN

P

93

TO HWY. 72

122

TO HWY. 119 & BOULDER

ROOSEVELT NATIONAL FOREST

118

Fourmile Canyon Road

TO BOULDER

52

Gold Hill Road

ROOSEVELT NATIONAL FOREST

89

Lickskillet Road to Lefthand Canyon

Gold Hill

89

Gold Hill Road

52

Gold Hill Road to Sunshine Canyon

Summerville

TO BOULDER

Grid size - 1/2 mile

MINI KEY

Paved
Easy
Moderate
Difficult
Other

89

MINI KEY
Paved
Easy
Moderate
Difficult
Other
Arapaho Nat'l Rec. Area
TO GRANBY, GRAND LAKE, & ROCKY MTN. NATIONAL PARK
40
Fraser
Rollins Pass
24
22
23
21
21
Winter Park
Tolland
25
Apex
Berthoud Pass
27
St.Marys Glacier
28
Alice
29
Fall River Road
275
26
Berthoud Falls
40
Empire
Central City
Blackhawk
EASY
MODERATE
DIFFICULT
70
TO GRAND JUNCTION
Ward
72
119
Nederland
Rollinsville
72
119
46
Golden Gate Canyon State Park
Pinecliffe
Eldorado Springs
Boulder
36
119
7
93
36
93
72
93
119
Idaho Springs
6
Golden
70
TO DENVER
Grid size - 5 miles

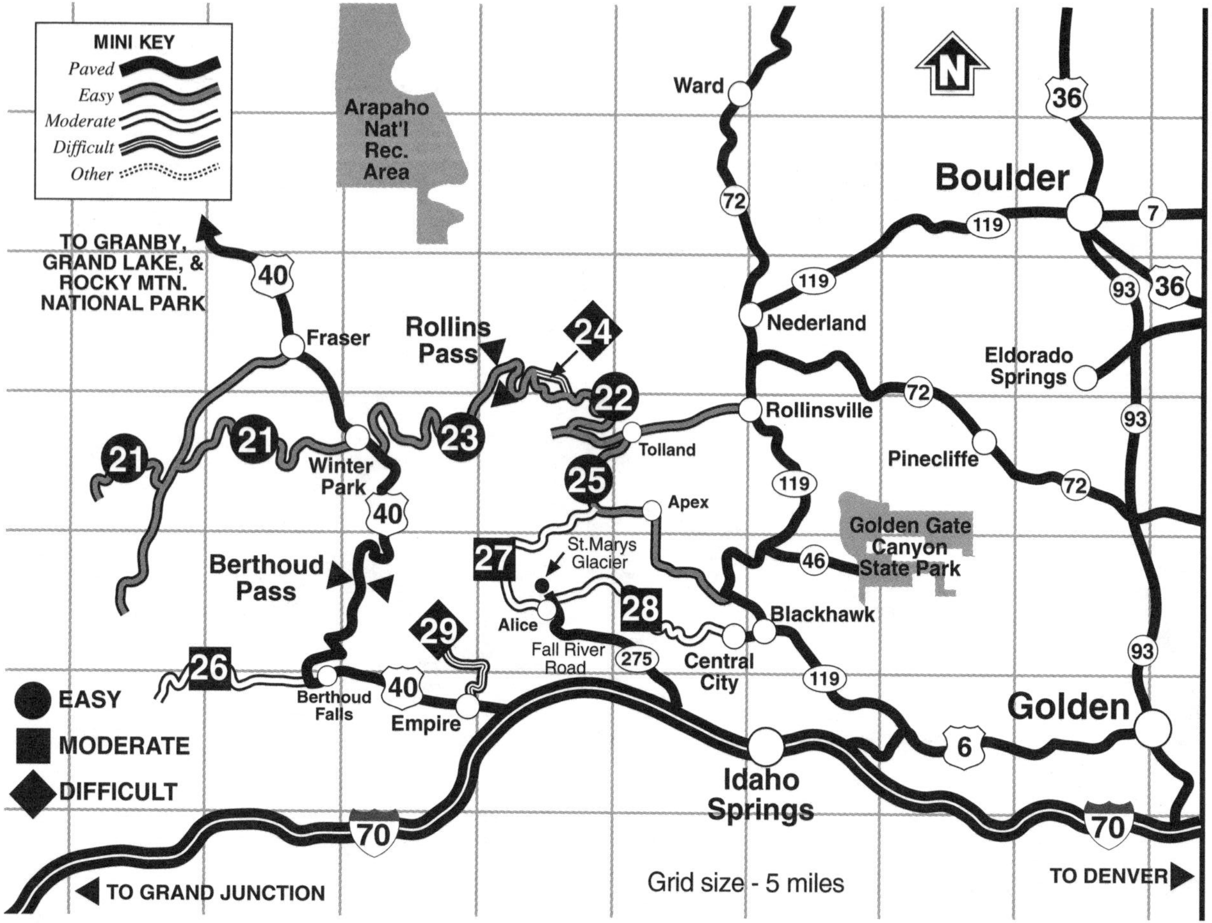

AREA 3

Winter Park, Central City, Rollinsville

21. Byers Peak
22. Rollins Pass East
23. Rollins Pass West
24. Jenny Creek Road
25. Apex Road
26. Jones Pass
27. Kingston Peak
28. Yankee Hill Road
29. Bill Moore Lake

Winter Park, Central City, Rollinsville

All of the trails in Area 3 are a short drive west of Denver on Interstate 70. Many of the trails are easy, scenic, and historically interesting. One of my favorites is Rollins Pass Road which has been blocked at the summit for several years following rock falls at the Needle's Eye Tunnel. Despite the fact that each side must be driven independently, this road is well worth your time. To enhance your trip, stop at the general store in Rollinsville and pick up a brochure entitled, *The Moffat Road,* which explains the road's fascinating history. On the way to Rollinsville, you'll pass Blackhawk and Central City. Although thousands of people visit these exciting gambling towns every day, few are aware that a relaxing break awaits them on backroads just outside of town. West of Central City, there is a network of roads enticing one to explore old mines and century-old cemeteries. For simplicity, I've selected one route through this area which I call Yankee Hill Road (Trail #28). It terminates at St. Mary's Glacier after a circuitous and moderately challenging adventure through hilly backcountry.

Rollins Pass Road East Side (Trail #22). Looking down on Yankee Doodle Lake.

91

Hiking trail to Byers Peak starts at a parking area at the end of F.S. 111.

The view of Byers Peak is somewhat limited by the trees with a few exceptions like this.

This photo was taken from St. Louis Creek Road just outside of Fraser.

Byers Peak ㉑

Location: West of Winter Park.

Difficulty: Easy. Suitable, under dry conditions, for any stock sport utility vehicle. Numerous spur roads make route-finding difficult.

Features: A complex network of easy roads close to the town of Winter Park and the Winter Park Ski Area. Many roads double as cross-country ski trails and snowmobile trails in the winter. Much of the trip passes through the Fraser Experimental Forest.

Time & Distance: As described here, it is about 17 miles from the town of Winter Park to the Byers Peak Hiking Trailhead. The return trip down St. Louis Creek Road to the town of Fraser is 13 miles. Allow 2 to 3 hours driving time for the entire trip. Allow extra time in case you get lost.

To Get There: Take Interstate 70 west from Denver to US 40. Follow signs north on US 40 over Berthoud Pass to the town of Winter Park. Once in town, turn left on well-marked Vasquez Road.

Trail Description: Reset your odometer when you turn off US 40 onto Vasquez Road. After 1.0 miles, the paved road goes right and is marked as Van Anderson Drive. Go straight at this point on Forest Service Road 148. The road is a little rocky but easy. At 2.0 miles, go straight through a seasonal gate. Bear right uphill on F.S. 159 at 2.5 miles. At 4.2 and 4.3 miles bear right at unmarked forks. At 5.0 miles, bear left following signs to St. Louis Creek Road. A right turn here would take you to Fraser.

At 6.7 miles, there is a sign indicating you are entering a research area. This is the Fraser Experimental Forest. You must stay on the road at all times through this area. Camping is allowed only in the Byers Creek and St. Louis Creek F.S. Campgrounds. At 7.1 miles, F.S. Rd. 159 goes right on a more direct route to St. Louis Creek Road. Bear left here on F.S. 163. At 8.9 miles, F.S. 162 crosses 163. Go straight through this intersection, staying on 163. It swings to the left after crossing 162. At 9.6 miles, you'll get your first good look at Byers Peak through the trees on the right. Bear right at 9.9 miles. Finally, at 10.9 miles, you reach St. Louis Creek Road 160. Turn left. After passing Byers Creek F.S. Campground, turn right on F.S. 164 at 12.0 miles. This road winds up the hill another 4.8 miles before reaching the Byers Peak Hiking Trail and parking area.

Return Trip: Turn around and head back down the same way you came up, however, this time, when you reach St. Louis Creek Road, turn left and follow it all the way to Fraser. You will pass the Fraser Experimental Station and the St. Louis Creek Campground. Bear right as you come into Fraser on what becomes Norgren Road. It swings left and runs into Eisenhower Drive. Turn right and cross the railroad tracks to US 40 in 0.2 miles. Right on US 40 takes you back to Winter Park. Left takes you to Granby.

Services: Full services in Winter Park and Fraser. There are pit toilets at the Byers Creek and St. Louis Creek F.S. Campgrounds.

Other Activities: Check with the Winter Park Chamber of Commerce for a schedule of summer activities (see Appendix for phone number). Camp at the two Forest Service campgrounds previously mentioned. Hiking and mountain biking trails are abundant. The Byers Peak Trail leads to a network of hiking trails into the Byers Peak Wilderness Study Area. If you hike to the the end of Byers Peak Trail, be prepared for a strenuous climb as the trail passes over talus slopes above timberline. You may also wish to drive to the end of St. Louis Creek Road to the St. Louis Creek Hiking Trail. In addition, you could continue south on Vasquez Road to the Vasquez Peak Wilderness Study Area. From there you can hike to Vasquez Pass on the Continental Divide. Don't forget the west side of Rollins Pass (Trail #23) departs just south of Winter Park on US 40.

Maps: Trails Illustrated Winter Park, Central City, Rollins Pass #103, Arapaho National Forest, Colorado Atlas and Gazetteer.

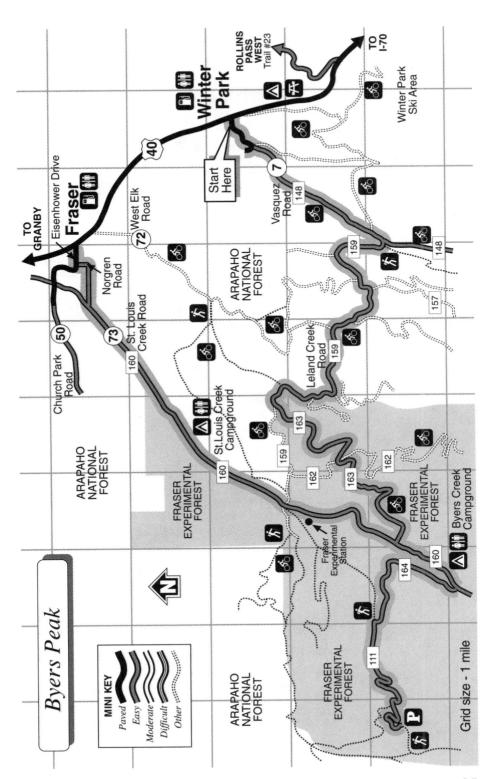

Byers Peak

MINI KEY
Paved
Easy
Moderate
Difficult
Other

N

Grid size - 1 mile

ARAPAHO NATIONAL FOREST

FRASER EXPERIMENTAL FOREST

ARAPAHO NATIONAL FOREST

FRASER EXPERIMENTAL FOREST

FRASER EXPERIMENTAL FOREST

Church Park Road

50

73

St. Louis Creek Road

160

St.Louis Creek Campground

160

159

163

162

162

163

159

164

160

Byers Creek Campground

111

P

Fraser Experimental Station

Norgren Road

TO GRANBY

Eisenhower Drive

Fraser

72

West Elk Road

40

Winter Park

Start Here

7

Vasquez Road

148

148

159

157

159

Leland Creek Road

ROLLINS PASS WEST Trail #23

TO I-70

Winter Park Ski Area

Road approaches the East Portal of the Moffat Tunnel and the start of Moffat Road.

Jenny Lake near the top, a rough but manageable quarter-mile detour from the main road.

Road ends here. Hike to the Needle's Eye Tunnel at far right. (Inset: close-up of tunnel.)

Rollins Pass East 22

Location: West of Rollinsville. North of Blackhawk.

Difficulty: Easy. Suitable, under dry conditions, for any stock sport utility vehicle and many passenger cars.

Features: Moffat Road, better known as the Rollins Pass Road, follows the course of an historically significant railroad route. It is one of the most popular backroads in Colorado despite the fact that the road is closed at the top, therefore, each side of the pass must be driven separately. (See Trail #23 for the west side.) Understanding the history of the railroad route will immensely enhance your trip. Inexpensive brochures for a self-guided auto tour, sponsored by the Rollins Pass Restoration Association, are available at many locations in the area and from the Forest Service offices in Boulder and Fort Collins. (See Appendix for phone numbers.)

Time & Distance: From Rollinsville, it's about 20 miles to the summit. Moffat Road begins at a fork near the East Portal of the Moffat Tunnel and continues for 12.2 miles to a point where the road is blocked. Allow 3 to 4 hours driving time for the round trip. Allow additional time to hike to the Needle's Eye Tunnel about a mile past the gate. A side trip to the East Portal of the Moffat Tunnel adds 1.4 miles.

To Get There: Take Highway 119 to the gambling town of Blackhawk which is reached from Interstate 70 west of Denver or via US 6 west of Golden. From Blackhawk, stay on Highway 119 north to Rollinsville and turn left on F.S. 149. Continue west 7.3 miles on this wide gravel road. A fork takes you left to the East Portal of the Moffat Tunnel or right to Rollins Pass.

Trail Description: *Reset your odometer at the start and begin the climb.* Views of the valley below can be seen as the road narrows and climbs quickly. The road switchbacks across the hill several times and is fairly wide in places. Note the eastern end of Jenny Creek Road (Trail #24) on the right at 5.5 miles. When you reach Yankee Doodle Lake at 9.4 miles, you'll see the western end of Jenny Creek Road. At 10.2 miles, a short, rocky spur road to Jenny Lake departs to the right. The last major switchback is at 11.1 as you pass the Forest Lakes Hiking Trailhead. Large boulders and a gate end this trip at 12.2 miles. The road is wide enough to turn around but just barely. To see the Needle's Eye Tunnel, hike another mile. As you walk, listen for the high-pitch chirping sounds of Colorado's favorite high-elevation rodent, the marmot.

Return Trip: Return the way you came.

Services: Rollinsville has a general store but no gas station. Closest gas can be found in Nederland about 4 miles north of Rollinsville on Highway 119. Otherwise, gas is available in Blackhawk. There is a Forest Service Campground and pit toilet about 1 mile north of Rollinsville on 119.

Other Activities: Rollins Pass Road is popular with mountain bikers because of its gentle grades, beautiful views, and relatively smooth road surface. There are many great places to hike, including two official trails near the summit. There is just one established picnic ground about 2.6 miles west of Rollinsville but you can stop just about anywhere, provided you stay clear of the road. Make sure you pack out all your trash.

Historical Highlights: As you roll along this road in your modern vehicle, try to imagine what events transpired to make your drive possible. Two centuries ago, Indians on horseback, then later Mormons in wagons, cut through this low point in the Continental Divide on their way from the Great Plains to points west. In 1873, a toll road was constructed by John Quincy Adams Rollins. The road quickly became a popular commercial route and the town of Rollinsville was born. Within a short time, however, Berthoud Pass replaced Rollins Pass as a more popular route. Not until 1903, when a wealthy dreamer by the name of David Moffat built a railroad up this mountainside, was commercial viability of the area restored.

The original plan for the railroad called for a 2.6 mile tunnel to be built near 10,000 ft. When money ran out, the rails were reluctantly laid over the pass at 11,660 ft. The railroad struggled for many years due to the incredible expense of keeping the route cleared of snow. A snowshed was built at the pass to help with the deepest snow which sometimes reached depths of thirty feet. The remains of this snowshed, a long ditch strewn with timbers, can still be seen at the summit on the west side trip (Trail #23). There are no traces, however, of the railroad station, hotel, and restaurant that existed here until 1928, made obsolete by the construction of the modern day 6.2 mile Moffat Tunnel built at a much lower altitude. Nineteen men died building the tunnel, which took over four years to complete. Trip time, however, was cut from 2 1/2 hours to 12 minutes.

Maps: Trails Illustrated Winter Park, Central City, Rollins Pass #103, Roosevelt National Forest, Colorado Atlas and Gazetteer.

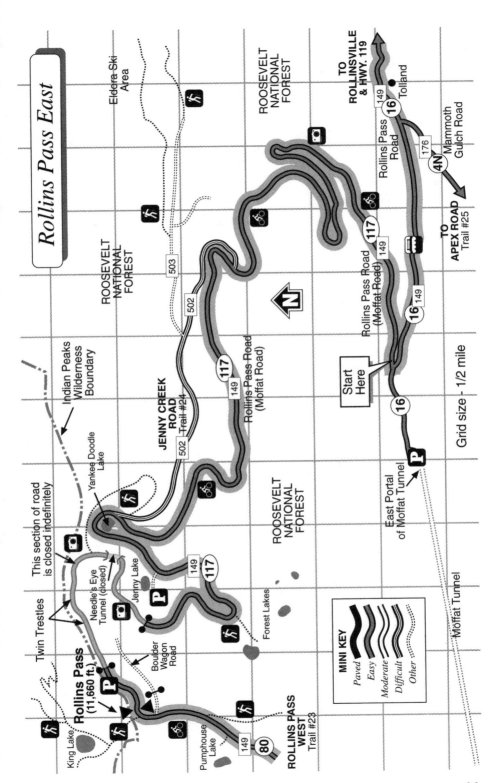

Rollins Pass East

Railroad trestle at the Rifflesight Notch. No need to hike, the road goes up to it.

The road is surprisingly smooth at the top. Winter Park Ski Area can be seen in the distance.

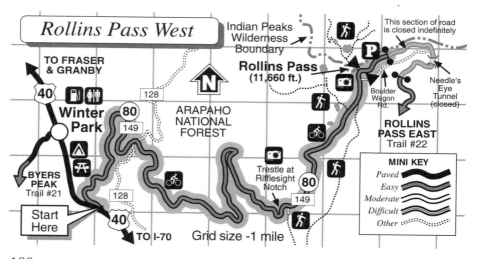

Rollins Pass West

Indian Peaks Wilderness Boundary

This section of road is closed indefinitely

Rollins Pass (11,660 ft.)

TO FRASER & GRANBY

40

128

N

ARAPAHO NATIONAL FOREST

Winter Park

80

149

Boulder Wagon Rd.

Needle's Eye Tunnel (closed)

ROLLINS PASS EAST Trail #22

BYERS PEAK Trail #21

128

Trestle at Rifflesight Notch

80

149

MINI KEY
Paved
Easy
Moderate
Difficult
Other

Start Here

40

TO I-70

Grid size -1 mile

Rollins Pass West ㉓

Location: East of Winter Park.

Difficulty: Easy. Suitable, under dry conditions, for any stock sport utility vehicle and many passenger cars.

Features: Rollins Pass Road follows an old railroad route used prior to the existence of the Moffat Tunnel and is of great historical interest. The Needle's Eye Tunnel just beyond the pass has been closed since 1990, consequently, each side of the pass must be driven independently. Efforts to reopen the tunnel in recent years have been unsuccessful.

Time & Distance: The road is 14.7 miles to the pass. Allow 2 to 3 hours driving time for the round trip.

To Get There: Take Interstate 70 west from Denver to US 40. Travel north on US 40 over Berthoud Pass. The entrance to Rollins Pass Road is across from the Winter Park Ski Area on the right about one mile before the town of Winter Park. A sign indicates *Moffat Road Hill Route*.

Trail Description: Route-finding is extremely easy. *Reset your odometer as you turn off US 40.* At 4.4 miles, go straight as you cross F.S. 128. You encounter the Rifflesight Notch Trestle at 11.0 miles. It's not necessary to hike to the trestle because the road goes up to it. Just before the pass at 14.7 miles, the old Boulder Wagon Road departs to the right. This four-wheel drive road is frequently closed. The main road ends at a parking area just beyond the pass.

Return Trip: Return the way you came.

Services: Full services in the town of Winter Park.

Other Activities: Hike the closed portion of the road to the Twin Trestles (see map on page 99). At one time you could drive over the trestles but they are now closed. See map for several other great hiking trails in the area.

Historical Highlights: See Rollins Pass East (Trail #22).

Maps: Trails Illustrated Winter Park, Central City, Rollins Pass #103, Arapaho National Forest, Colorado Atlas and Gazetteer.

I took this shot through my front windsheild where the trail follows the creek.

This spot is tougher than it looks. Note partial bridge lower left. F.S. 503 goes to the right.

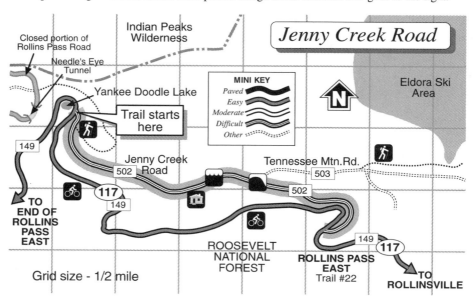

Jenny Creek Road 24

Location: West of Rollinsville. North of Blackhawk.

Difficulty: Difficult. Very narrow in places with several challenging rocky sections and stream crossings. Easier going downhill as described here. Not recommended for full-size vehicles. Creek may be deep in the spring.

Features: Provides a challenging alternative route to Rollins Pass Road.

Time & Distance: The trail is only 3.3 miles, but allow 1 to 2 hours.

To Get There: Follow directions to Rollins Pass East (Trail #22). When you reach Yankee Doodle Lake at 9.4 miles, you can see Jenny Creek Road on the right heading back down the mountain.

Trail Description: Reset your odometer as you turn right off Rollins Pass Road at Yankee Doodle Lake. As you head downhill, bear right at 0.2 miles. This open area is popular for camping. Drop down a steep, rocky section at 1.1 miles. Bear right at 1.5 and pass the remains of a cabin. Negotiate an off-camber section at 1.7 miles next to Jenny Creek. After that, the trail follows the creek bed. Bear left out of the stream at 1.8 miles. The next stretch winds in and out of the creek and passes through tight spots in the trees. The worst spot on the trail comes at 2.2 miles where you have to make a tight right turn over some large boulders then climb out of the creek over a deteriorated wooden bridge. At this point, F.S. 503 goes to the left down to some hiking trails into the Eldora Ski Area. Continue across the bridge and start climbing out of the valley. The road gets easier before you reach Rollins Pass Road at 3.3 miles. Don't short-cut up the side of the hill before you reach the end of the trail.

Return Trip: Bear left for Rollinsville.

Services: There is a general store in Rollinsville and gas at Nederland.

Other Activities: This trail is popular for hiking and extreme mountain biking. Camp along the upper portion of the trail where permitted.

Maps: Trails Illustrated Winter Park, Central City, Rollins Pass #103, Roosevelt National Forest, Colorado Atlas and Gazetteer.

This photo was taken from F.S. 353 looking west to the Continental Divide.

These old cabins in Apex are still used as residences. Stay on the road and pass quietly.

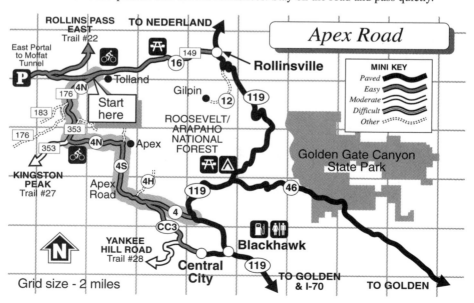

Apex Road 25

Location: Southwest of Rollinsville. Northwest of Blackhawk.

Difficulty: Easy. A rocky, washboard surface but wide most of the way. When dry, the road can be driven by any stock sport utility vehicle.

Features: A nice way to return from Rollins Pass East (Trail #22) to Central City and Blackhawk. Conversely, you can drive north from Central City. Explore other spur roads in the area.

Time & Distance: About 11 miles from the starting point described here to Highway 119 north of Blackhawk. Allow about 1 hour driving time.

To Get There: Follow directions to Rollins Pass East (Trail #22). Head west on F.S. 149 from Rollinsville about 5 miles. Just past the little town of Tolland, make a left on F.S. 176, also marked as County Rd. 4N.

Trail Description: *Reset your odometer as you turn left off Rollins Pass Road at Tolland.* You quickly climb up a rocky stretch of road with great views of Rollins Pass Road below. A spacious camping spot is at 1.5 miles on the right. After that, F.S. 183 and F.S. 176 go to the right. You continue straight on what becomes F.S. 353. Go straight again at 2.3 miles. At 3.5, bear left on Apex Road as 353 goes right to Kingston Peak (Trail #27). Continue straight at a cattle guard at 3.7 miles. A sign indicates you are entering the Arapaho National Forest. When you reach the town of Apex at 5.8 miles, turn right. At 9.0 miles, bear left for highway 119. (A right turn, at this point, would take you to Central City.) After passing through a long residential area, you reach Highway 119 at 11.3 miles.

Return Trip: At Highway 119 turn left for Rollinsville. Right takes you downhill to Blackhawk, Interstate 70, or Golden.

Services: There is a general store in Rollinsville but no gas. Return to Blackhawk for gas and other services.

Other Activities: Golden Gate Canyon State Park, where numerous campgrounds and picnic areas are available, is just east of Highway 119.

Maps: Trails Illustrated Winter Park, Central City, Rollins Pass #103, Roosevelt and Arapaho National Forests, Colorado Atlas and Gazetteer.

The road comes up through this valley past the Henderson Mine Complex in center of photo.

Looking up at the Continental Divide. Jones Pass is the low point at the left.

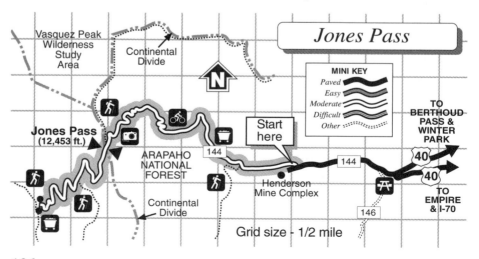

Jones Pass 26

Location: West of Empire. Southwest of Berthoud Pass.

Difficulty: Moderate. This rating is based not so much on the road surface, but rather on the high elevation (12,453 ft.) and the remote nature of the trail. Any mechanical problems below the pass on the west side would be serious if you are traveling alone because the only way out is back up the mountainside. If you descend the west side, travel with another vehicle.

Features: A relatively good road surface for a pass at this high altitude. Beautiful views can be seen in all directions from the top. Not heavily traveled despite its easy access from Denver and surrounding areas.

Time & Distance: About 6 miles to the top of the pass from US 40. Add another 3 miles if you descend the west side all the way to the bottom. Allow 2 to 3 hours for the entire round trip.

To Get There: Take Interstate 70 west from Denver to US 40. Travel north on 40 about 7.4 miles past the town of Empire. Turn left on F.S. 144 just after the little town of Berthoud Falls. The Big Bend Picnic Ground is on the left. The first 1.6 miles is paved until you reach the Henderson Molybdenum Mine Complex. Just before the gated entrance to the mine, turn right on a gravel road. This is the starting point.

Trail Description: Reset your odometer at the start. At 0.6 miles, a sign indicates four-wheel drive required. There are a few minor spur roads along the way but the main road is obvious to Jones Pass at 4.2 miles. You may continue about 3 more miles on good road down the west side of the pass. There is an old mine and hiking trail at the bottom.

Return Trip: Return the way you came.

Services: Gas and restrooms are available in Empire.

Other Activities: You can hike all the way to Winter Park across the Continental Divide and eventually connect with another trail to Vasquez Road. (See Byers Peak, Trail #21.)

Maps: Trails Illustrated Winter Park, Central City, Rollins Pass #103, Roosevelt and Arapaho National Forests, Colorado Atlas and Gazetteer.

Near timberline, this SUV stops beside the trail northeast of Kingston Peak.

Most of the road above timberline is rocky. A few places are worse than this.

Snow blocks the toughest part of the trail. Longs Peak can be seen on horizon, upper right.

Kingston Peak 27

Location: Between St. Mary's Glacier and Rollinsville.

Difficulty: Moderate. One of the more challenging moderate trails because of several steep, rocky sections at the top. As described here, however, these sections are driven downhill. If you drive the trail in the opposite direction, assume a difficult rating. I drove this trail in early October just after the first snowfall and the toughest part of the trail was partially snow-covered. Consequently, I was not able to drive about one mile of the trail at the top. I hiked this portion and inspected it as best I could. To complete the trail, I descended and drove all the way around to Rollinsville. From there, I drove up the other side. I had to estimate the mileage for the portion of the trail I couldn't drive, so my mileages may be off slightly for the northern part of the trip. I don't recommend you drive the trail when I did. The best time is in August and early September before it snows. In the spring, the wooded, northeastern portion of the trail often remains snow covered until late June or early July. Don't drive this trail alone.

Features: This route crosses a large, relatively flat area above timberline. Views are spectacular in every direction. Several fourteeners can be seen from the top including Longs Peak to the north and Mt. Evans to the south. Immedialtely west is James Peak at 13,294 ft. On a clear day, you can see Interstate 70 and Georgetown to the south. Bring your camera and a pair of binoculars.

Time & Distance: It's about 8 miles from the start of the trail west of Alice to where the trail joins Apex Road (Trail #25). Allow 2 to 3 hours driving time for the trail plus considerable time to get there and return. There are many spur roads on the northern side that lead to a large network of trails southeast to Central City. Should you decide to explore this area, allow all day. It is very easy to get lost in this network.

To Get There: Take Interstate 70 west from Denver to Fall River Road Exit 238. Follow signs to the St. Mary's Glacier. Drive north on Fall River Road 275 about 8 miles to Alice Road on the left marked by a row of mailboxes. *Reset your odometer at this point.* Head west on Alice Road 0.1 miles and turn right on Silvercreek. At 0.4 miles turn left on Texas Drive. At 0.9 miles, turn right uphill on Nebraska. It switchbacks to the left and then right before it intersects with Hillside Road at 1.1 miles. Turn left on Hillside and at 1.3 miles, turn right up the hill on Hilltop Road. This is the start of the trail. (Street signs may not be in place, so watch your mileages carefully.)

Trail Description: *Reset your odometer.* Hilltop Road soon becomes F.S.
353. The trail gets rougher as it climbs above timberline and then levels out
across a wide plateau. There is a steep, rocky descent at 2.5 miles before a
final climb up Kingston Peak. The highest point is reached at 4.0 miles at an
elevation over 12,000 ft.

   The next half mile is the toughest part of the trail as it descends down
the other side of the mountain. After that it gets much easier. At 6.4 miles
F.S. 175 goes to the right. You bear left. Bear left again at 6.7 and 7.7 miles.
At 8.0 miles, F.S. 353 runs into Apex Road.

Return Trip: At Apex Road, you have two options: turn right and follow
directions for Apex Road (Trail #25) to Highway 119 or continue straight to
Rollins Pass Road County Rd. 16 where a right turn takes you to
Rollinsville.

Services: If you are driving the trail in the direction described here, the
closest gas station is in Blackhawk or Central City. If you are driving the
trail in the opposite direction, Idaho Springs is your closest full-service
location.

Other Activities: You can continue north a short distance on Fall River Road
past the town of Alice to the St. Mary's Glacier Ski Area. This direction also
takes you past the west end of Yankee Hill Road (Trail #28). You can head
up this way and explore many spur roads in the area. Just be careful—it's
easy to get lost.

   There is a network of hiking trails west of Kingston Peak. This is serious hiking country because much of it is above timberline. One of the trails
goes over Rogers Pass and eventually reaches Rollins Pass West (Trail #23)
at the Rifflesight Notch Area.

Maps: Trails Illustrated Winter Park, Central City, Rollins Pass #103,
Roosevelt and Arapaho National Forests, Colorado Atlas and Gazetteer.
*Special note: None of these maps accurately depicts every spur road in this
area. If you decide to explore other roads, you'll need a compass and an
excellent sense of direction. Make sure you have plenty of gas, water, food,
and blankets in case you get lost overnight.*

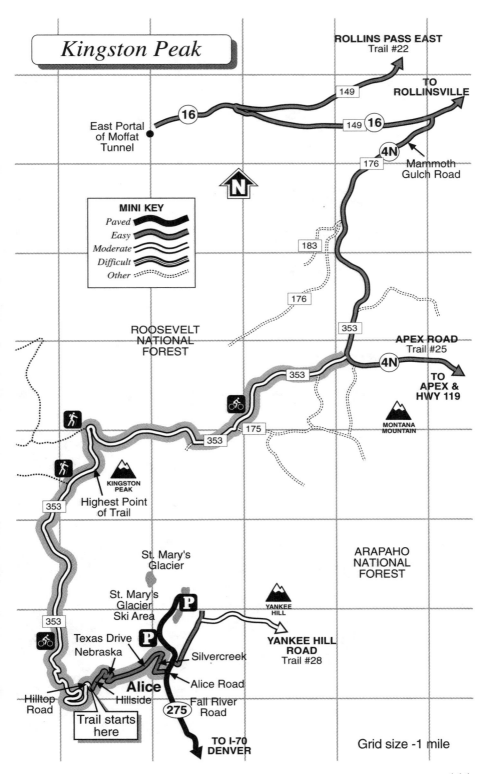

Kingston Peak

ROLLINS PASS EAST
Trail #22

149

TO ROLLINSVILLE

149 16

16

East Portal
of Moffat
Tunnel

4N

176

Mammoth
Gulch Road

N

MINI KEY
Paved
Easy
Moderate
Difficult
Other

183

176

353

APEX ROAD
Trail #25

ROOSEVELT
NATIONAL
FOREST

353

4N

**TO
APEX &
HWY 119**

175

**MONTANA
MOUNTAIN**

353

**KINGSTON
PEAK**

353

Highest Point
of Trail

St. Mary's
Glacier

**ARAPAHO
NATIONAL
FOREST**

353

St. Mary's
Glacier
Ski Area

P

**YANKEE
HILL**

Texas Drive

P

Nebraska

Silvercreek

**YANKEE HILL
ROAD**
Trail #28

Alice Road

Alice

Hilltop
Road

Hillside

Fall River
Road

275

Trail starts
here

**TO I-70
DENVER**

Grid size -1 mile

111

St. Mary's Glacier as seen from Yankee Hill.   Yankee Hill Road descends to Fall River Rd.

This cemetery marks the start of the trip.

Much of the road is easy, as shown here, but there are several tough sections along the way.

Yankee Hill Road

Location: Between Central City and St. Mary's Glacier.

Difficulty: Moderate. There are just a few rocky sections on this trail that require a moderate rating. Much of the trail is easy. Route-finding, however, is very confusing. There is a complex network of roads in the area. My map shows only a portion of the spur roads that exist. Don't depend on route markers. They may be vandalized or changed by the time you read this. Make sure you have plenty of gas, water, food, and warm clothing in case you get lost. I also recommend you carry a compass and as many maps as possible. The best map I have found is the Trails Illustrated Map noted at the end of this section. It, too, shows only a portion of spur roads, but topographic information provides another tool to help orient yourself.

Features: On the way to the start of the trail, you'll pass through historic Blackhawk and Central City, two former mining towns now known for gambling. The end of the trail offers spectacular views of the St. Mary's Glacier Ski Area.

Time & Distance: The entire trip from Central City to Fall River Road is about 11 miles. Assume 2 to 3 hours driving time one way. Allow plenty of extra time in case you get lost.

To Get There: Follow signs to Blackhawk via Interstate 70 west from Denver or US 6 from Golden. A well marked intersection in Blackhawk takes you left to Central City. Pass through the heart of Central City and continue west as a one-way street changes back to two-way. Less than a mile west of town, turn left at an intersection following signs to the Columbine Campground. Immediately, make another left and you should see the Rocky Mountain Cemetery on the right (see photo on opposite page).

Trail Description: Reset your odometer to zero at the Rocky Mountain Cemetery as you proceed. There is a picnic area with a pit toilet on the left just past the cemetery. Bear right at 1.5 miles on F.S. 273.2, Bald Mountain Road. At 1.7, bear left at the Bald Mountain Cemetery. Bear left at 3.4 miles as F.S. 401.1 goes to the right. Go straight when you reach an unmarked road that comes in from the left before reaching a complex intersection at 3.6 miles. Turn right at this intersection following F.S. 175.1. At 3.7 miles go straight as F.S. 739.1 goes to the right. Turn left when you encounter a private gate at 4.7 miles as the road begins to narrow. After passing through a rough spot by a crossbuck fence, turn right on F.S. 175.3. This road bypasses a rougher section that goes straight uphill marked as F.S. 175.3B. Bear left at an unmarked intersection at 6.1 miles. Through a complex intersection at 6.3 miles, continue straight into the trees up the steepest and roughest looking trail marked as F.S. 175. This stretch of road is the most difficult part of the trip. At 6.7 miles, bear left following F.S. 175.3. Bear left at the next four intersections at 7.1, 7.3, 7.9, and 8.2 miles. After that you reach the crest of the hill and begin to descend. At 8.4 miles, F.S. 271.1 goes left; you go right on F.S.175.4. Go straight at 8.9 miles staying on 175.4. At 9.1 you can pull over and view St. Mary's Glacier.

Continue downhill and bear left at 9.5 miles before running into Mine Road at 9.6 miles. Turn left downhill on Mine Road passing several roads that depart to the right. Mine Road finally runs into Fall River Road at 10.1 miles.

Return Trip: Turn left on Fall River Road and follow pavement down to Interstate 70. Left at Interstate 70 takes you back to Denver. Follow signs to the freeway.

Services: Full services available in Idaho Springs.

Other Activities: This area is popular for hikers and mountain bikers. Skiing is possible well into summer at the St. Mary's Glacier Ski Area.

Historical Highlights: Central City and Blackhawk have become thriving boom towns once again, this time as a result of legalized gambling. Over a century ago, a boom of another sort occurred. When gold was discovered here in massive amounts, the two cities grew at a record-breaking pace. In the early 1860s, Central City was known as the "richest square mile on earth." Not to be outdone, Blackhawk became known as "the mill city of the rockies" as it processed ore for all the mining towns in the area, including Central City, Nevadaville, Gregory, Nederland, and Rollinsville. One might think that the two cities would be staunch supporters of each other, however, the opposite is true. Since the early days when Central City sent its malodorous waste downstream to Blackhawk, the two cities have been competitors. The competition continues today as some visitors, bound for Central City, find no reason to continue beyond Blackhawk. Ironically, as both cities prosper, the past is being preserved through the restoration of historic buildings funded by profits from gambling.

Maps: Trails Illustrated Winter Park, Central City, Rollins Pass #103, Roosevelt and Arapaho National Forests, Colorado Atlas and Gazetteer.

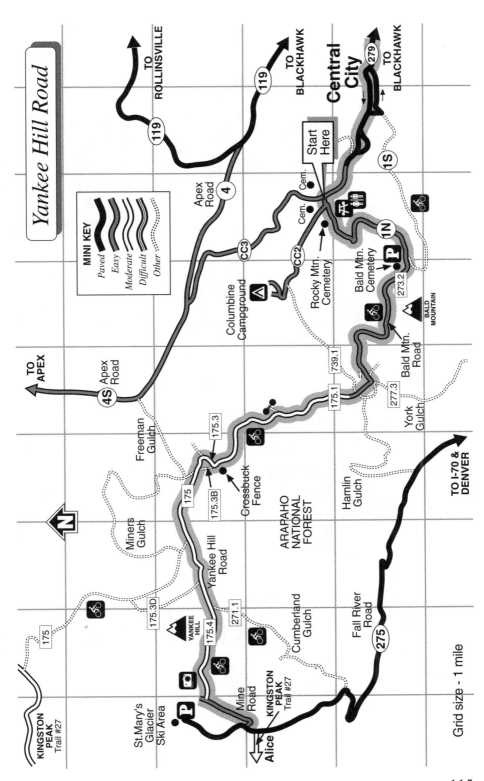

Yankee Hill Road

MINI KEY
Paved
Easy
Moderate
Difficult
Other

TO ROLLINSVILLE
TO BLACKHAWK
119
119
TO BLACKHAWK
279
TO BLACKHAWK
Central City
Start Here
1S
Cem.
Cem.
1N
P
273.2
BALD MOUNTAIN
Bald Mtn. Cemetery
Rocky Mtn. Cemetery
Bald Mtn. Road
York Gulch
277.3
739.1
175.1
Apex Road
4
CC3
CC2
Columbine Campground
Freeman Gulch
Apex Road
TO APEX
4S
175.3
175
175.3B
Crossbuck Fence
Miners Gulch
N
Yankee Hill Road
ARAPAHO NATIONAL FOREST
Hamlin Gulch
TO I-70 & DENVER
Fall River Road
275
Cumberland Gulch
175.3D
175.4
YANKEE HILL
271.1
KINGSTON PEAK
Trail #27
Mine Road
Alice
P
St.Mary's Glacier Ski Area
175
KINGSTON PEAK
Trail #27

Grid size - 1 mile

115

Bill Moore Lake is nestled high against the Continental Divide.

Empire below, Georgetown in the distance.

Typical loose, steep section near the top.

The toughest part of the trail begins after the Conqueror Mine, shown here.

Bill Moore Lake 29

Location: North of Empire.

Difficulty: Difficult. The upper portion of the trail has several steep, loose rocky sections. Although many stock sport utility vehicles make it all the way to the lake, the climb is not for the faint-of-heart. The trip is easier if your vehicle is equipped with differential lockers. Stock SUVs can enjoy beautiful high-elevation scenery by avoiding the uppermost portion of the trail. Conversely, those looking for greater challenge, can find it on several spur roads in the area.

Features: Like so many places in Colorado, mining played a major role in the area's development. There are several well-preserved mines along the route, most notably, the Conqueror Mine, shown on the opposite page. (See Historical Highlights.)

Time & Distance: It is 5.7 miles from the start of the trail as shown here to Bill Moore Lake. Allow 1 to 2 hours one way.

To Get There: Take Interstate 70 west from Denver to US 40. Travel north on 40 about 1.4 miles to the town of Empire. Turn right at the main intersection in Empire marked as North Empire Road. The road is paved but quickly becomes dirt. Go about 0.7 miles and bear right at a fork where F.S. 261.1 goes left. This is the start of the trail.

Trail Description: Reset your odometer at the start and begin to climb. Bear right at 0.4 miles as the road gets narrower and rougher. There are beautiful views of the valley to your right. You can see Georgetown and Guanella Pass on a clear day. The road appears to end at 1.6 miles as you reach a gate and the Conqueror Mine. However, the road continues sharply uphill to the right. Try to go up the hill as straight as possible to avoid getting too off-camber. After this point, the road becomes quite narrow with increasing undulations. Continue straight at 1.9 miles as a road to the left shortcuts the switchback. Bear right at 2.2 and again at 2.4 where a sign indicates you are entering the Arapaho National Forest.

You reach a Forest Service gate at 2.5 miles. A sign here indicates Bill Moore Lake is to the left and Miller Creek Gulch is right. Bear left again at 2.7 and 3.1 miles. After crossing an off-camber rocky section, the trail comes out of the trees before reaching a three-way intersection at 3.4 miles. Forest Service Road 171.3C goes downhill to the right. Make a sharp left up a steep undulating road surface marked as F.S. 183.1. Immediately bear left again as 183.1A goes right. At 3.5 miles, you climb the first of several steep, loose, rocky sections. Stock vehicles will find these sections very challenging. Bear left at 4.0 miles as 183.1C goes right. You soon reach a high point and start back downhill. At 4.7 and 4.9 miles bear right staying on 183.1. The trail narrows into the trees as you drop steeply downhill before finally reaching Bill Moore Lake at 5.7 miles.

Return Trip: At one time, you could exit this area by connecting with Mill Creek Road to the east, however, that trail has been closed to vehicular traffic. To exit the area, you must go out the same way you came in.

Services: Gas and restrooms are available in Empire.

Other Activities: There are no established hiking trails in the area other than the road itself. The rugged terrain draws only the hardiest of mountain bikers.

Historical Highlights: The town of Empire enjoyed a long and prosperous life as one of the earliest gold camps in Colorado. Most people are not aware, however, that there was another mining town about 1 mile north of Empire. The road leading up to the town is the first part of the trail described here. This town, known as North Empire, prospered during the 1860s and 70s. Many of the men who lived in North Empire worked in the highly productive Conqueror Mine. Getting up and down the mountain was always a challenge because the railroad terminated at Empire. Several boarding houses were built in North Empire to reduce the need to go down the mountain. One company built a smaller cable-operated railroad, but horse and wagon remained the primary means of transportation. Only traces of North Empire remain today.

Maps: Trails Illustrated Winter Park, Central City, Rollins Pass #103, Roosevelt and Arapaho National Forests, Colorado Atlas and Gazetteer.

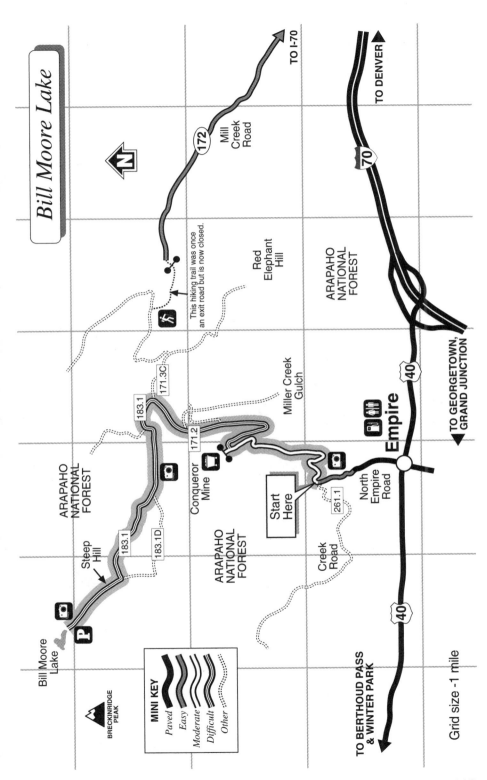

Bill Moore Lake

N

TO I-70

172 Mill Creek Road

TO DENVER

70

This hiking trail was once an exit road but is now closed.

Red Elephant Hill

ARAPAHO NATIONAL FOREST

171.3C

183.1

171.2

Miller Creek Gulch

ARAPAHO NATIONAL FOREST

Conqueror Mine

183.1

183.1D

Steep Hill

Empire

North Empire Road

261.1

Start Here

Creek Road

TO GEORGETOWN, GRAND JUNCTION

40

40

TO BERTHOUD PASS & WINTER PARK

Bill Moore Lake

P

BRECKINRIDGE PEAK

MINI KEY

Paved
Easy
Moderate
Difficult
Other

Grid size -1 mile

AREA 4

Steamboat Springs,
Hahns Peak,
Columbine

30. Ellis Jeep Trail
31. Hahns Peak
32. Farwell Mountain
33. Blowdown Area
34. Buffalo Pass

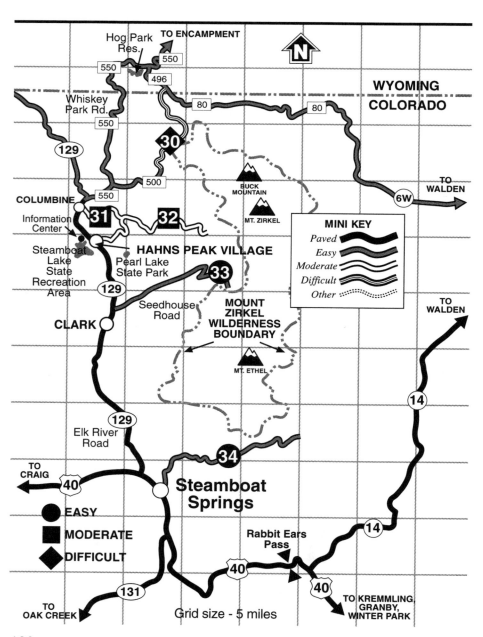

Steamboat Springs, Hahns Peak, Columbine

Roads in this part of the state are at relatively low elevations compared to other parts of Colorado. The highest point reachable by four-wheel drive vehicle, of the roads described here, is Farwell Mountain at 10,824 ft. (Trail #32). Higher mountains, including Mt. Zirkel at 12,180 ft., are located inside the Mt. Zirkel Wilderness Area where no vehicular traffic is allowed. Nonetheless, the area offers several distinct backcountry experiences including a very easy drive to the Blowdown Area (Trail #33), where freak winds have flattened over four million trees. If you drive Ellis Jeep Trail (Trail #30), make sure to go with another vehicle because frequent mudholes are not always within winching distance of the nearest tree. Explore a maze of old mining roads encircling distinctive Hahns Peak (Trail #31). While in the Hahns Peak area, step back in time with a stop in Columbine where you can rent a secluded cabin and learn the best places to fish, hunt, and hike. Visit Steamboat Lake State Recreation Area, Pearl Lake State Park, and Hahns Peak Lake which have facilities for picnicking, camping, and fishing.

Hahns Peak, with its distinctive volcanic shape, serves as a landmark for the area.

The trail gets slick after a heavy rain.

Large mudholes await the unwary.

This stock Grand Cherokee was able to negotiate much of the trail.

Ellis Jeep Trail ◆30◆

Location: North of Steamboat Springs and Columbine.

Difficulty: Difficult. If you are a hard-core four-wheeler looking for ultimate rock challenges, you might be a little disappointed with this trail. The trail would receive a moderate rating if it weren't for several open meadows that are wet and muddy most of the time. It's easy to get stuck and trees are not always within reach of a winch cable. You should travel with another vehicle so each can provide an anchor point for the other. Mud terrain tires are certainly a benefit. It rained heavily the day I drove the trail except for the last couple of miles. I managed to make it through without getting stuck, but used my differential lockers several times to keep all four tires turning.

Features: The first part of the trail weaves up and down tightly through the forest then levels out as it crosses several long meadows. Part of the trail follows the western border of the Mt. Zirkel Wilderness Area. The end of the trail leaves you far from any services and actually crosses the state border into Wyoming.

Time & Distance: The trail is 9.5 miles long from the starting point I've indicated on the map. Allow at least 2 hours one way. You should add considerable time to return.

To Get There: Take Interstate 70 west from Denver to US 40. Travel north on 40 to Steamboat Springs. After passing through Steamboat Springs, turn right on Elk River Road County Rd. 129. Follow 129 north past the Steamboat Lake State Recreation Area. About 1/2 mile past the small town of Columbine, turn right on Whiskey Park Road, F.S. 550. *Reset your odometer at this point.* At 3.7 miles turn right on Red Park Road F.S. 500. Continue on 500 as the road narrows at 6.3 miles. At 8.1 miles, follow the road as it turns sharply to the left before it meets F.S. 500.1A at 8.4 miles. This is the start of the trail.

Trail Description: Reset your odometer. At the start of the trail, F.S. 500.1A goes to the right. You go straight staying on F.S. 500. Bear left at 0.5 and 2.7 miles as the road gets rougher. At 2.8 miles, the road levels out as you pass through the trees. Watch for a sign on the right for Ellis Jeep Trail, F.S. 499. The sign explains that the road follows the border of the Mt. Zirkel Wilderness Area and that no motorized travel is allowed east of the road.

Bear right here, following the road downhill into the forest. F.S. 500 continues to the left as it follows the Continental Divide for a few more miles and eventually becomes a hiking trail.

As you continue on F.S. 499, you soon pass the remains of a cabin on the right. The road descends, then climbs steeply in places. There are some narrow spots but full-size vehicles can get through if they take their time. Eventually you exit the main part of the forest and begin crossing a series of meadows. As you encounter muddy sections, stay on the road. Attempting to bypass the mudholes will further damage the terrain. There are several small stream crossings along the way that may be deep in the spring. You pass through another heavily wooded section before reaching F.S. 82 at 7.1 miles. Turn left. After passing through a gate at 9.1 miles, bear left as 82.1A goes right. You reach the end of the trail at 9.5 miles as it meets County Rd. 6B (same as F.S. 80).

Return Trip: The shortest way back to Steamboat Springs is to return the way you came over the trail. An easier way is to drive farther north into Wyoming to Hog Park Reservoir. From there, you can connect to Whiskey Park Road F.S. 550 back to County Rd. 129 and Columbine. To return to the front range, a distance of about 150 miles, take F.S. 80 east which connects to County Road 6W into Cowdrey. Head south to Walden on C.R. 125. From Walden take C.R. 14 east to Fort Collins. Make sure you have a statewide Colorado road map before you embark in this direction.

Services: There is a small store near Hahns Peak Village that has a couple of gas pumps. Otherwise, fill up in Steamboat Springs before heading north. You are a long way from a gas station at the end of the trail so make sure you have plenty of gas before you start. Gas is available in Walden, about 50 miles east on the return route described above.

Other Activities: Steamboat Springs is a fabulous winter ski resort. However, it is also great in the summer, offering hiking, biking, horseback riding, camping, fishing, and boating. Three excellent camping areas include Pearl Lake State Park, Steamboat Lake State Recreation Area, and the smaller Hahns Peak Lake. Steamboat Lake is large with great boating and fishing. There are two campgrounds around the lake. The Bridge Island Campground, where one of two boat ramps is located, has a new laundry facility with clean, modern restrooms and showers. Stop in at the Information Center north of the lake.

Maps: Trails Illustrated Hahns Peak, Steamboat Lake #116, Routt National Forest, Medicine Bow National Forest (Wyo.), Colorado Atlas and Gazetteer. A Colorado and Wyoming state map are also helpful.

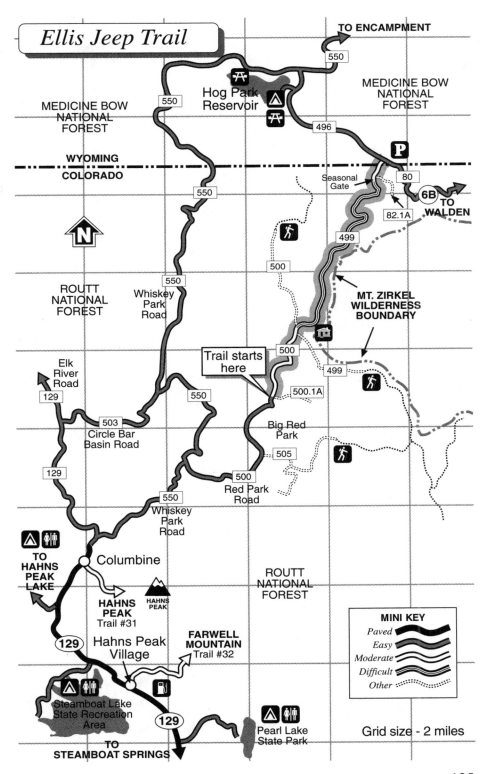

Ellis Jeep Trail

TO ENCAMPMENT

550

MEDICINE BOW
NATIONAL
FOREST

Hog Park
Reservoir

550

496

P

MEDICINE BOW
NATIONAL
FOREST

MEDICINE BOW
NATIONAL
FOREST

WYOMING

COLORADO

550

Seasonal
Gate

80

82.1A

6B
TO
WALDEN

N

499

500

MT. ZIRKEL
WILDERNESS
BOUNDARY

ROUTT
NATIONAL
FOREST

550

Whiskey
Park
Road

550

500

Trail starts
here

550

500.1A

499

Elk
River
Road

129

503

Circle Bar
Basin Road

550

Big Red
Park

505

129

500

Red Park
Road

550

Whiskey
Park
Road

TO
HAHNS
PEAK
LAKE

Columbine

HAHNS
PEAK
Trail #31

HAHNS
PEAK

ROUTT
NATIONAL
FOREST

129

Hahns Peak
Village

FARWELL
MOUNTAIN
Trail #32

MINI KEY

Paved
Easy
Moderate
Difficult
Other

Steamboat Lake
State Recreation
Area

129

Pearl Lake
State Park

Grid size - 2 miles

TO
STEAMBOAT SPRINGS

Looking down from F.S. 490A to F.S. 490. An overcast day partially obstructs the view.

There is a wide place to park near the top but you must hike from here to the summit.

Hahns Peak

Location: North of Steamboat Springs. East of Columbine.

Difficulty: Moderate. The trail is rocky and steep in places. The upper roads are narrow with some tight switchbacks. Careful driving is required. More aggressive stock sport utility vehicles should have no problem with the main trail described here. Explore side trails at your own risk.

Features: A short trail that climbs near the top of Hahns Peak. There are great views of the surrounding area along the way including Steamboat Lake. An extensive network of old mining roads in the area can be explored. Ratings for side roads are not specified.

Time & Distance: Just under 4 miles from Highway 129 at Columbine to the parking area at the top of Hahns Peak. This part of the trip takes less than 1 hour. If you continue to Farwell Mountain (Trail #32), add an additional 3 miles and another 1/2 hour.

To Get There: Take Interstate 70 west from Denver to US 40. Travel north on 40 to Steamboat Springs. After passing through Steamboat Springs, turn right on Elk River Road County Rd. 129. Drive 29 miles north past the Steamboat Lake State Recreation Area to the small town of Columbine. Watch for F.S. 490 on the right. This is the starting point.

Trail Description: Reset your odometer at the start. The trip begins on an easy gravel road as it passes several cabins. At 1.0 miles bear left as F.S. 410 goes to the right back to Hahns Peak Village. Bear right at 1.4 miles as F.S. 418 continues uphill. (You can hike to the top of Hahns Peak by continuing on 418 about another 0.5 miles to a hiking trail that goes up the northwest side of the Peak.) There is a small stream crossing at 1.5 miles. At 1.8 miles bear right as an unmarked road goes up the hill to the left. Bear left at 2.1 miles as F.S. 410B goes right. Views begin to appear as you climb on a rocky but manageable road. Go straight at 2.3 miles as 417 goes right. At 2.5 miles bear left as 490B goes right. Finally, at about 3.0 miles, the road widens just a bit. To the left is a narrow shelf road marked as 490A which takes you to the top of Hahns Peak. The first part of the road is very narrow but it widens somewhat as you continue to the top. After several tight switchbacks, you reach a wide area at 3.9 miles where you can park and hike to the top. At one time you could drive down the other side of the peak, but that trail is closed.

To continue to Farwell Mountain (Trail #32), head back down 490A. *Reset your odometer when you reach 490.* Turn left and begin your descent down the east side of Hahns Peak. Turn right at 0.7 miles onto F.S. 414. The road alternately climbs and falls as it zig-zags through the trees on a fairly rocky road. At 2.0 miles, turn right again as 413B goes to the left. At this point, you cross the Ellis Creek Hiking trail. You reach Farwell Mountain Road at 2.9 miles. Bear left for Farwell Mountain.

Return Trip: Return the way you came or by the first part of Farwell Mountain Road (Trail #32). After a rain, this part of Farwell Mountain Road can be very slick and muddy. I don't recommend this route under wet conditions.

Services: There is a store just south of Hahns Peak Village with restrooms and a couple of gas pumps. You can also get gas in Clark. Otherwise, return to Steamboat Springs for full services. An Information Center with restrooms is located near the main entrance to Steamboat Lake on Hwy. 129. Pit toilets are located at Hahns Peak Lake, Steamboat Lake, and Pearl Lake, but a fee is required for day-use.

Other Activities: Many people enjoy hiking to the top of Hahns Peak either by following the route described here or by hiking up a trail on the northwest side. This hiking trail is accessed from F.S. 418, described earlier, however, you can also hike any of the side roads. This was once a very active mining area. Be careful around old mine sites. It is best to view them from a distance. Never let children play around mines.

Historical Highlights: Like many other places in Colorado, Hahns Peak was once a booming mining area. Hahns Peak Village was the county seat between 1879 and 1912 and grew to a population of over 500 people. The volcanically formed Hahns Peak was named after Joseph Hahn, a prospector who discovered gold here in the early 1860s. During a particularly harsh winter in 1866, his supplies ran out. Hahn attempted to snowshoe over 100 miles to the town of Empire but died of starvation before reaching his destination.

Maps: Trails Illustrated Hahns Peak, Steamboat Lake #116, Routt National Forest, Colorado Atlas and Gazetteer.

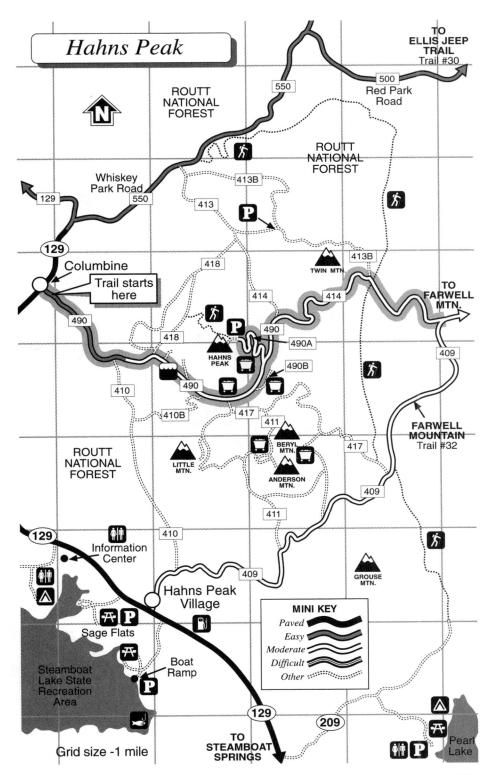

Hahns Peak

TO ELLIS JEEP TRAIL Trail #30

ROUTT NATIONAL FOREST

550

500

Red Park Road

N

ROUTT NATIONAL FOREST

Whiskey Park Road

413B

129

550

413

P

129

Columbine

Trail starts here

490

418

414

413B

TWIN MTN.

414

414

TO FARWELL MTN.

409

P

490

490A

418

HAHNS PEAK

490B

490

410

417

490

410B

411

490

FARWELL MOUNTAIN Trail #32

LITTLE MTN.

BERYL MTN.

417

ANDERSON MTN.

409

411

410

ROUTT NATIONAL FOREST

409

GROUSE MTN.

129

Information Center

Hahns Peak Village

MINI KEY

Paved

Easy

Moderate

Difficult

Other

Sage Flats

Boat Ramp

Steamboat Lake State Recreation Area

129

209

Pearl Lake

Grid size -1 mile

TO STEAMBOAT SPRINGS

Pearl Lake State Park as seen from the top of Farwell Mountain on a foggy day.

The first half of the trip is easy when dry. If wet, the surface of the road is extremely slick.

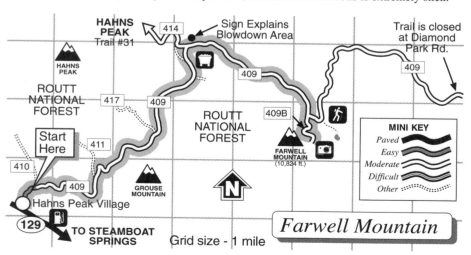

HAHNS PEAK
Trail #31

414

Sign Explains
Blowdown Area

Trail is closed
at Diamond
Park Rd.

HAHNS
PEAK

409

409

ROUTT
NATIONAL
FOREST

417

409

409

409B

ROUTT
NATIONAL
FOREST

FARWELL
MOUNTAIN
(10,824 ft.)

Start
Here

411

GROUSE
MOUNTAIN

N

MINI KEY

Paved
Easy
Moderate
Difficult
Other

410

409

Hahns Peak Village

129

TO STEAMBOAT
SPRINGS

Grid size - 1 mile

Farwell Mountain

Farwell Mountain 32

Location: North of Steamboat Springs. East of Hahns Peak Village.

Difficulty: Moderate. The upper part of the trail is fairly rocky and steep in places. Stock, high-clearance SUVs will be able to get through with some effort. The lower part is easy when dry, but if wet, the road becomes extremely slick. Use caution on sidehills to avoid sliding off the road.

Features: Crosses gentle pastures then climbs to great views.

Time & Distance: About 9.7 miles one way to the top of Farwell Mountain. Allow 2 to 3 hours for the round trip.

To Get There: Take Interstate 70 west from Denver to US 40. Travel north on 40 to Steamboat Springs. After passing through town, turn right on Elk River Road County Rd. 129. Drive about 25 miles north to Hahns Peak Village. Turn right at Main Street F.S. 409. This is the start.

Trail Description: Reset your odometer at the start. Drive east through town and bear right at 0.8 miles. Turn left at a private gate at 1.0 miles. This spot can be very muddy if wet. At 1.7 miles, bear right as F.S. 411 goes left. Bear left at 5.2 miles. The trail gets rougher, and at 5.5 miles it intersects with F.S. 414 which goes left to Hahns Peak (Trail #31). Bear right and pass a sign for the Blowdown Area. The road becomes quite rocky and steep for a while. At 8.8 miles, bear right on F.S. 409B and climb a rutted but gentle grade to the top. Trees in the area appear to have suffered a forest fire sometime in the past. You start downhill after passing radio towers. Stop before the road begins to descend steeply.

Return Trip: Return the way you came or via F.S. 414 to Hahns Peak (Trail #31). At one time you could continue on 409 to Diamond Park Road but that exit is now closed because of the Blowdown.

Services: Gas and restrooms are available south of Hahns Peak Village and in Clark. Otherwise, head back to Steamboat Springs for full services.

Other Activities: Explore several spur roads into the Hahns Peak Area.

Maps: Trails Illustrated Hahns Peak, Steamboat Lake #116, Routt National Forest, Colorado Atlas and Gazetteer.

This is just one small portion of the devastation seen immediately south of F.S. Road 443.

Large trees have been entirely uprooted.

A closer view from hiking trail.

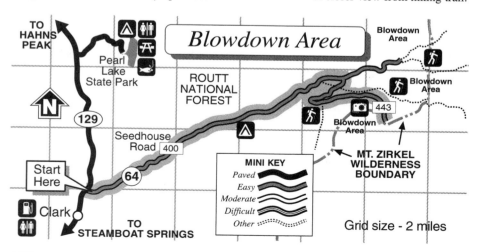

Blowdown Area

TO HAHNS PEAK

Pearl Lake State Park

ROUTT NATIONAL FOREST

Blowdown Area

Blowdown Area

Blowdown Area

129

Seedhouse Road 400

Start Here

64

Clark

TO STEAMBOAT SPRINGS

MT. ZIRKEL WILDERNESS BOUNDARY

443

MINI KEY
Paved
Easy
Moderate
Difficult
Other

Grid size - 2 miles

Blowdown Area ③③

Location: North of Steamboat Springs. Northeast of Clark.

Difficulty: Easy. A wide gravel road suitable for all SUVs.

Features: This road has been selected because it is one of the best places to view the Blowdown Area.

Time & Distance: About 12.6 miles one way. Allow 1/2 hour to reach the viewing area near the end of F.S. 443.

To Get There: Take Interstate 70 west from Denver to U.S. 40. Travel north on 40 to Steamboat Springs. After passing through town, turn right on Elk River Road County Rd. 129. Drive north past the town of Clark and turn right on Seedhouse Road marked as County Rd. 64 and F.S. 400.

Trail Description: Reset your odometer as you turn east onto Seedhouse Road. Drive 9.5 miles and turn right on F.S. 443. Follow this washboard road as it turns west for a distance and then back to the east. At 12.6 miles the road widens somewhat near the Three Island Lake Trailhead. Pull over and park here. There are good views of the blowdown area to the south.

Return Trip: Return the way you came.

Services: Return to Steamboat Springs.

Other Activities: Many side roads and campgrounds in the area are closed for safety reasons. (Call Blowdown Hotline for status. See Appendix for phone number.) Although hiking in the area is discouraged, it is not prohibited. You may travel at your own risk. I hiked the Three Island Lake Trail without difficulty and was able to get some great close-up views. There were many other people on the trail.

Historical Highlights: Over four million trees were toppled on October 25, 1997 by freak easterly winds in excess of 120 miles per hour. Spruce and fir trees, with shallow root systems, are accustomed to westerly winds and could not sustain strong winds from the east. A few trees will be cleared, but most of the forest will be left as is. Eventually the forest will regrow.

Maps: Routt National Forest, Colorado Atlas and Gazetteer.

Looking west from near the pass. Much of the road is wide and smooth, as shown here.

Wildflowers line the road at various places along the way.

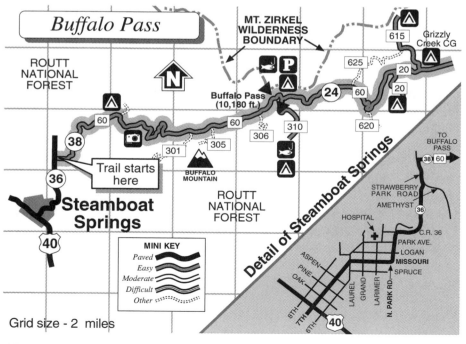

Buffalo Pass

MT. ZIRKEL
WILDERNESS
BOUNDARY

ROUTT
NATIONAL
FOREST

615   Grizzly
       Creek CG

625   20

N

Buffalo Pass
(10,180 ft.)

24   60   20

60   60   310

306   620

301   305

Trail starts
here

BUFFALO
MOUNTAIN

36   Steamboat

ROUTT
NATIONAL
FOREST

38

40   Springs

MINI KEY
Paved
Easy
Moderate
Difficult
Other

Grid size - 2 miles

TO
BUFFALO
PASS

38   60

STRAWBERRY
PARK ROAD

AMETHYST   36

HOSPITAL

Detail of Steamboat Springs

C.R. 36

PARK AVE.

LOGAN

MISSOURI

SPRUCE

ASPEN

PINE

OAK

LAUREL
GRAND
LARIMER
N. PARK RD.

8TH
7TH
6TH

40

134

Buffalo Pass ③④

Location: Northeast of Steamboat Springs.

Difficulty: Easy. Suitable, when dry, for most sport utility vehicles.

Features: This road was once an important route between Steamboat Springs and Walden. It now serves as a quiet backcountry getaway to several Forest Service Campgrounds and fishing lakes.

Time & Distance: About 20 miles from the start to Grizzly Creek Campground. Allow 1 hour in each direction.

To Get There: Take Interstate 70 west from Denver to US 40. Travel north on 40 to Steamboat Springs. Turn right on 7th St. and go four blocks to a 4-way stop. Cross through the intersection and bear slightly right on Missouri. After three blocks the road goes left and becomes N. Park Rd. Three more blocks takes you right on Cty Rd. 36. After the road swings north, it meets Amethyst Drive. Continue north less than a mile to F.S. 60 on the right.

Trail Description: *Reset your odometer as you turn east onto F.S. 60.* The pavement ends quickly and at 3.3 miles you pass the Dry Lake Campground. After passing through a seasonal gate, the road narrows a little. Ignore several smaller roads that go right until reaching the summit at 11.0 miles. Turn right at a parking area then make an immediate left following signs to Grizzly Creek Campground. At 17.5 miles, turn left as F.S. 620 goes right. Go straight at 19.3 as F.S. 20 goes right. Go straight again at 20.2 as F.S. 615 goes left. Grizzly Creek C.G. is on the left at 20.3 miles.

Return Trip: Return the way you came or continue east another 11 miles to Highway 14 which will take you southwest to Steamboat Springs or northeast to Walden.

Services: Full services in Steamboat Springs.

Other Activities: There are many easy side roads in the area that connect to a variety of fishing lakes. They include at least five lakes at the summit, in addition to Fish Creek Reservoir, Hidden Lake, and Teal Lake.

Maps: Trails Illustrated Clark, Buffalo Pass #117, Routt National Forest, Colorado Atlas and Gazetteer.

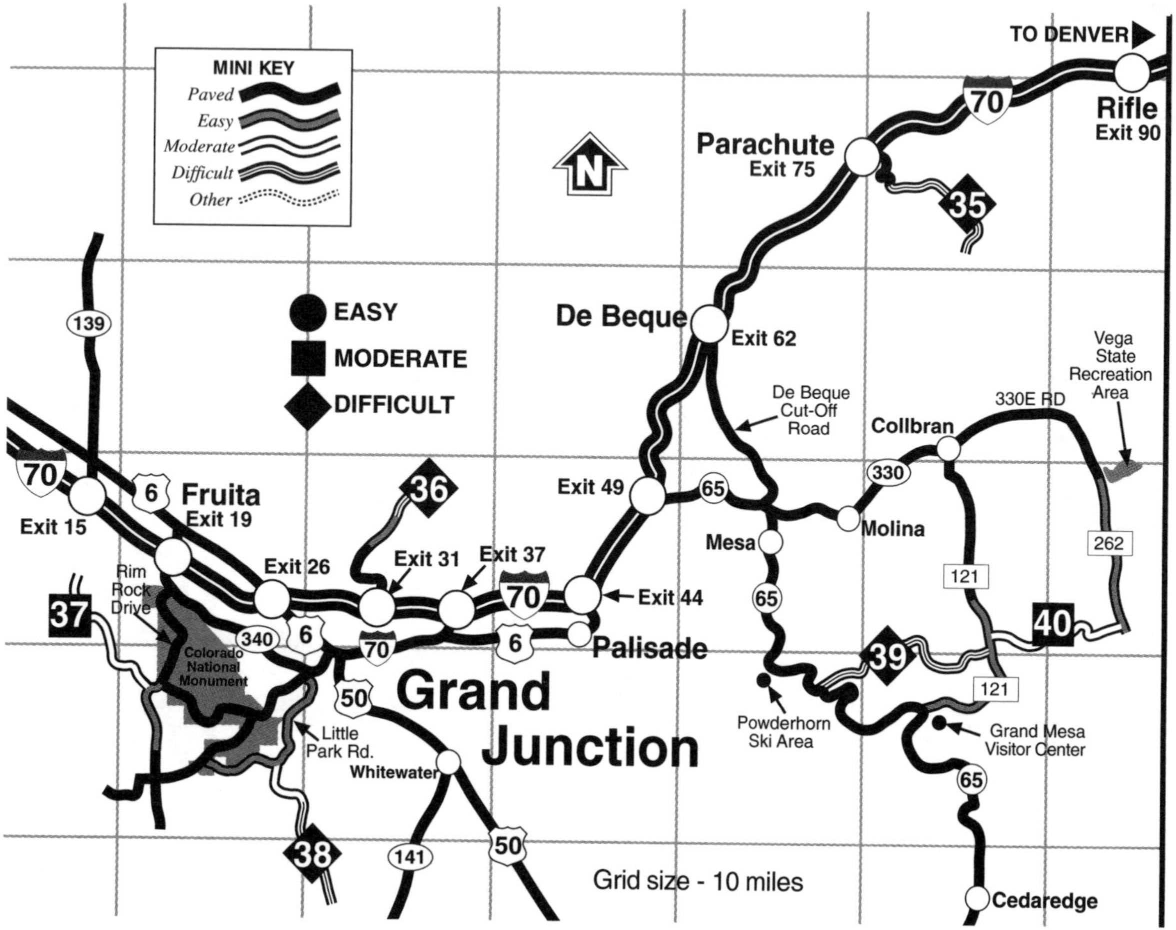

AREA 5

Grand Junction,
Battlement Mesa

35. Battlement Mesa
36. Grand Junction Desert
37. Rattlesnake Canyon
38. Bangs Canyon
39. Long Slough
    Reservoir Road
40. Kenney Creek
    Reservoir Road

MINI KEY
Paved
Easy
Moderate
Difficult
Other

EASY
MODERATE
DIFFICULT

TO DENVER
Rifle
Exit 90

Vega State
Recreation
Area

330E RD

Parachute
Exit 75

De Beque
Cut-Off
Road

De Beque
Exit 62

Collbran

Molina

Grand Mesa
Visitor Center

Cedaredge

Mesa

Powderhorn
Ski Area

Exit 44

Palisade

Exit 49

Grand
Junction

Exit 37

Exit 31

Whitewater

Little
Park Rd.

Exit 26

Fruita
Exit 19

Colorado
National
Monument

Rim
Rock
Drive

Exit 15

Grid size - 10 miles

136

Grand Junction, Battlement Mesa

This area has a variety of trail conditions, all quite different than other parts of Colorado. Bangs Canyon (Trail #38), offers solid traction on wind-carved rocks reminiscent of Utah's Moab area. Pass through the Colorado National Monument on your way to spectacular Rattlesnake Canyon (Trail #37). Grand Junction Desert (Trail #36) is open BLM land where you are permitted to drive anywhere over long expanses of roller coaster-like terrain. This trail is rated difficult based on its tougher sections, but much of the area is easy to moderate. Long Slough Reservoir Road (Trail #39) is located high on the Grand Mesa where thick vegetation and tenacious mud sometimes create jungle-like conditions. Battlement Mesa (Trail #35) is the best known of all the trails in the area. It has a long-time reputation for satisfying the most avid four-wheeler. Rumors of the trail's demise because of Forest Service improvements have been greatly exaggerated. Although the worst mud bogs at the summit have been blocked and bypassed, the remainder of the trail, including the torturous *Rock Garden*, is still intact.

Photo taken from the trailside as it skirts the eastern end of Rattlesnake Canyon (Trail #37).

The start of the trail is straight ahead. A parking area is to the left.

A portion of the *Rock Garden*. This stretch of rocks is more difficult than it looks.

Stay to the right across this meadow to avoid deep holes and the need for a winch.

A new bypass road has been built around the deepest mud bogs, seen at left.

Battlement Mesa 35

Location: Northeast of Grand Junction. Southeast of Parachute.

Difficulty: Difficult. Do not drive this trail by yourself. It is a punishing trip for the most capable, modified vehicle. Differential lockers, mud terrain tires, and high ground clearance are highly recommended. Most of the time the trail is a diabolical mix of slick mud and large boulders which throw your vehicle from side to side against tightly spaced trees. During drier months, some of the mud changes to a fine dust that hangs in the air and sticks to everything. The trail is easier when dry. The worst of the boulder fields is called the *Rock Garden*. Fortunately, it has a bypass which is so well used it appears to be the main trail. The deep mud bogs near the end of the trail have been closed and a bypass has been constructed around this area. Other smaller mud bogs, however, remain a challenge for the balance of the trail. Mosquitoes are plentiful during warmer summer months, so bring insect repellent.

Features: It is a long, dusty drive to the start of the trail marked by a large parking area. The trail climbs for its entire length, at times very steeply. It reaches an elevation of about 10,000 ft. It finally levels off at an open and attractive area around the Battlement Reservoirs.

Time & Distance: The trail is just barely over 4 miles in length but allow at least 3 to 4 hours for the round trip. If you are traveling with a group and go through the *Rock Garden*, it will take considerably longer.

To Get There: Take Interstate 70 to Parachute (Exit 75). Head south and cross the Colorado River. After about 0.7 miles from the freeway, turn right on West Battlement Mesa Parkway. You'll pass a golf course on the left before West Battlement Mesa changes to South Battlement Mesa. Watch for Stone Quarry Road on the right at about 1.4 miles. Turn right here and go about 0.3 miles past the cemetery. Turn left on Underwood Road just after the cemetery and head east on a wide gravel road. Continue straight as the road begins to climb and wind through an area that appears to have been destroyed by a forest fire some time ago. After traveling more than 6 miles past the cemetery, you encounter a series of cattle guards that mark private property. The property owners have been kind enough to allow you to cross their land, so please pass through quietly and courteously and stay on the main road at all times. Within 0.3 miles of the fourth and last cattle guard, there is a wide parking area. The trail departs straight ahead on the right.

Trail Description: *Reset your odometer at the start.* Within a short time, the trail becomes rocky and narrow as it alternates through pine and aspen groves. At 0.7 miles you reach a rocky fork. Left takes you through the difficult *Rock Garden*. Getting through without lockers is a real challenge and body damage is likely. The lengthy obstacle is tougher than it looks.

Another fork is reached at 1.8 miles. Bear right up a steep grade. This climb is followed by an open meadow before heading back into the trees. Another meadow at 2.7 miles should be approached carefully. Deep holes on the left of the trail can suck you in unexpectedly. I helped winch a large truck after it dropped steeply into a hole causing a front tire to come off its rim (see photo). At 3.2 miles, you drop down a steep rocky section called *Hell's Gate*. This section is followed by what used to be a series of gigantic mud bogs. The Forest Service has blocked the area with fallen trees and built a bypass around the left side (see bottom photo page 138). There are still several smaller bogs to cross before reaching the end of the trail at 4.1 miles. A picturesque reservoir marks the end of the trail.

Return Trip: Return the way you came.

Services: Return to the town of Parachute for full services. The small town has several restaurants, hotels, and gas stations. There is also a self-service car wash south of the freeway exit.

Other Activities: The trail is predominantly used by four-wheelers and ATVers but occasionally you will see a hiker or back-packer along the road. Give them a wide berth. There is also an equestrian trail that departs from the parking area at the start of the trail.

Maps: White River National Forest, Colorado Atlas and Gazetteer. No Trails Illustrated map covers this area.

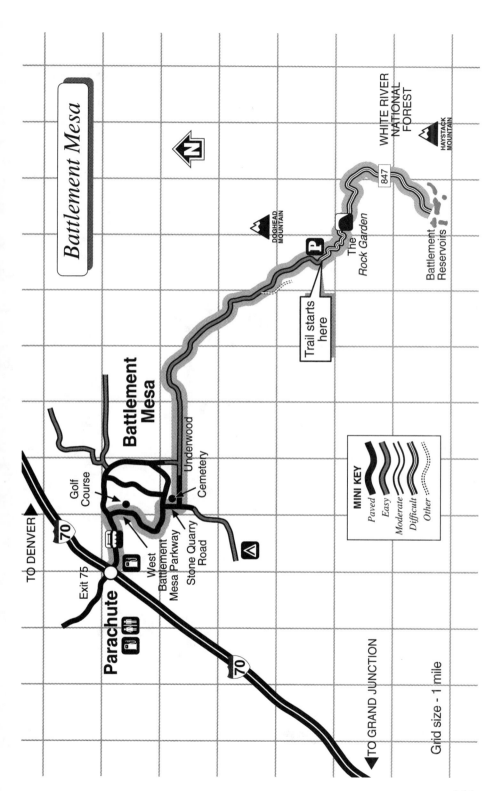

Battlement Mesa

TO DENVER

Parachute

Exit 75

West
Battlement
Mesa Parkway

Golf Course

Battlement Mesa

Stone Quarry Road

Underwood Cemetery

70

TO GRAND JUNCTION

DOGHEAD MOUNTAIN

Trail starts here

P

The *Rock Garden*

847

WHITE RIVER NATIONAL FOREST

HAYSTACK MOUNTAIN

Battlement Reservoirs

MINI KEY

Paved
Easy
Moderate
Difficult
Other

N

Grid size - 1 mile

141

The Book Cliffs form a natural boundary on the northeast.

This is just one small portion of the entire area. Trails run in all directions.

Blazing a new trail is allowed.

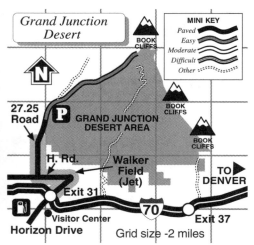

Grand Junction Desert

MINI KEY
Paved
Easy
Moderate
Difficult
Other

BOOK CLIFFS

N

27.25 Road

P

GRAND JUNCTION DESERT AREA

BOOK CLIFFS

BOOK CLIFFS

H. Rd.

Walker Field (Jet)

TO DENVER

Exit 31

70

Exit 37

Visitor Center

Horizon Drive

Grid size -2 miles

Grand Junction Desert ◆36◆

Location: Immediately north of Grand Junction.

Difficulty: Difficult. This rating is based on just a portion of the area. There are many miles of easy and moderate terrain to explore. Use caution on steep slopes and off-camber hillsides. Know the capability of your vehicle, and drive slowly over hilltops.

Features: This is open BLM land. You are permitted to drive anywhere within the boundaries of the area. When dry, the soil is soft and dusty, not sandy. I do not recommend using the area when wet. It becomes muddy and slippery. The mud dries like cement on your vehicle.

Time & Distance: Time and distance are at the discretion of the driver. You can easily spend a day exploring the area.

To Get There: Take Interstate 70 to Grand Junction and get off at Horizon Drive, Exit 31. Head north less than a mile and turn left just before Walker Field at the jet plane on display. Head west on "H" Road about a mile and turn north on 27 1/4 Road. Turn right at several entry points along the way. West of 27 1/4 Road, travel is restricted to existing roads

   To find the difficult area shown in the pictures at left, continue north on 27 1/4 Road until the pavement ends. Bear right at the next two forks before reaching some telephone poles which are less than 2 miles from the pavement. Head east a short distance before reaching a steep embankment. Look for a reasonable entry point.

Trail Description: You may drive anywhere within a triangular-shaped area of approximately 18 square miles. The area is defined by 27 1/4 Road on the northwest and the Book Cliffs on the northeast. The southern boundary is an irregular line of private land north of Interstate 70.

Return Trip: Return the way you came, or, at the eastern end of the area near Interstate 70 Exit 37.

Services: Full services in Grand Junction.

Maps: BLM Grand Junction Resource Area Map, Colorado Atlas and Gazetteer.

A small part of the scenery inside the Colorado National Monument.

This was the toughest spot on the road at the time this photo was taken.

A stock SUV crosses the eastern end of Rattlesnake Canyon near the end of the road.

A hiker begins his descent down to the arches in Rattlesnake Canyon. It's a long, tough hike.

Rattlesnake Canyon

Location: East of Grand Junction and the Colorado National Monument.

Difficulty: Moderate. Parts of the lower access road are rocky. However, with careful tire placement, any stock sport utility with good ground clearance will have no problem. There were several stock SUVs parked at the end of the road. The upper access road was closed when I was there in October, so I was not able to rate this road myself. Local sources tell me the upper road is very similar in difficulty to the lower road.

Features: Rattlesnake Canyon is accessed via Black Ridge Road which has an upper section and a lower section. The lower section is open between August 15 and February 15. The upper section is open between April 15 and August 15. Both routes are closed February 15 through April 15. Check with the Bureau of Land Management (see Appendix) for any unscheduled closures. Late summer and fall are the best times to visit this area. In mid summer, insects are a nuisance and temperatures often climb above 100 degrees.

Time & Distance: From the start of Black Ridge Road to the end of the trail is about 10.7 miles. Allow about 3 hours for the round trip. Plan some additional time to hike down to the Rattlesnake Arches. Also allow adequate time to drive through the Colorado National Monument.

To Get There: Take Interstate 70 to Fruita (Exit 19) west of Grand Junction. Head south on Highway 340 about 2.4 miles and turn right on Rim Rock Drive into the Colorado National Monument. Pass through a toll booth and pay a daily use fee if you plan to visit the entire park. If you are just passing through to reach the trail, tell the guard where you're going. He may waive the fee. Travel through the park about 10.8 miles and turn right at a sign for the Glade Park Store. Go 0.2 miles and turn right again for the start of the trail. A sign here says "Welcome to Black Ridge."

Trail Description: Reset your odometer at the start. The road begins by winding through a small valley on a hard-packed clay surface. When dry, the road is easy, but be careful if wet. The clay can become slippery. At 1.3 miles, the upper road goes left and the lower road goes right. Only the lower road is described here. Go right, and at 1.6 miles turn left at a gate. The road weaves its way up and down across Black Ridge with beautiful views of the Grand Valley below. There are a few rocky places but nothing too tough. At 8.4 miles, bear right as the upper road comes in from the left to rejoin the lower road. As you head downhill, you encounter the toughest part of the trail. A little washed-out area forces you to stay to the right at 9.3 miles. Go slow, place your tires carefully, and you should have no problem. Possible maintenance on the trail may have improved this spot. The road soon passes the eastern end of Rattlesnake Canyon where you can look down and see the full length of the Canyon. If you look straight down and to the right, you can see deep circular cuts in the canyon walls. These cuts are actually arches. You have to hike down to see them completely. The end of the trail is reached at 10.7 miles and is marked by a parking area and a sign for the hiking trail. From here you can hike to the arches.

Return Trip: Return the way you came.

Services: Full services in Grand Junction and Fruita.

Other Activities: Camping is allowed along the roadside but not along the hiking trail or near the arches. A close-up view of the arches is worth the hike. Only Utah's Arches National Park has a higher concentration of arches. The hike is fairly long and strenuous, so you must be in good condition and acclimated to Colorado's dry, thin air. Take along plenty of water, especially during the hot summer months. Don't forget your camera.

Rim Rock Drive through the Colorado National Monument is 22 miles long and continues past the point where you turned off. The park consists of over 18,000 acres of spectacular rock formations and high cliffs. Don't miss Miracle Rock, weighing over 12,000 tons, and supposedly the largest balanced rock in the world. You can exit at the opposite end of the park from which you entered. The park is open all year.

Maps: BLM Grand Junction Resource Area Map, Colorado Atlas and Gazetteer.

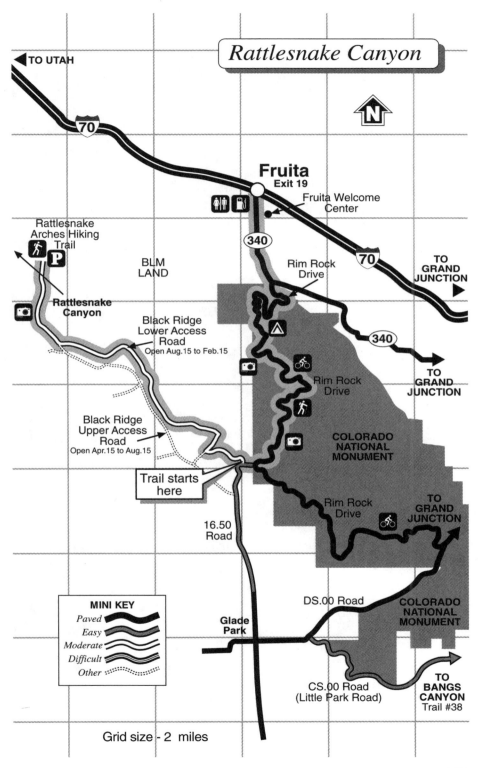

Rattlesnake Canyon

TO UTAH

N

70

Fruita
Exit 19

Fruita Welcome
Center

340

Rattlesnake
Arches Hiking
Trail

P

BLM
LAND

Rim Rock
Drive

70

TO
GRAND
JUNCTION
►

**Rattlesnake
Canyon**

Black Ridge
Lower Access
Road
Open Aug.15 to Feb.15

340

TO
GRAND
JUNCTION

Rim Rock
Drive

Black Ridge
Upper Access
Road
Open Apr.15 to Aug.15

**COLORADO
NATIONAL
MONUMENT**

Trail starts
here

Rim Rock
Drive

TO
GRAND
JUNCTION

16.50
Road

MINI KEY
Paved
Easy
Moderate
Difficult
Other

DS.00 Road

**COLORADO
NATIONAL
MONUMENT**

**Glade
Park**

CS.00 Road
(Little Park Road)

TO
BANGS
CANYON
Trail #38

Grid size - 2 miles

The start of the trail is well marked.

It's narrow in places and slippery if wet.

The first part of the trail descends along this monolithic ridge.

The second half of the trip is fairly rough in spots but there are no major obstacles.

Bangs Canyon ◆38◆

Location: Southwest of Grand Junction.

Difficulty: Difficult. The beginning of the route descends on a wide rock slab to the bottom of Rough Canyon over terrain of varying difficulty. Easy and moderate choices are available for stock SUVs on this part of the trail. The road becomes more defined as it climbs up the other side of the canyon, however, difficult sections cannot be bypassed. Adventurous drivers with stock vehicles will need high ground clearance and excellent articulation to continue on this part of the trail.

Features: The scenery is quite spectacular and draws heavy traffic at times. The area is closely monitored by the Bureau of Land Management for environmental impact. Many of the side roads are already under consideration for closure. However, the course described here is scheduled to stay open, provided users remain responsible. Please obey all signs, stay on the designated trails, and follow *Tread Lightly* guidelines. This trail is a popular biking and hiking area, so be courteous to everyone. When appropriate, pull over and let others pass.

Time & Distance: The portion described here is 4.7 miles one way. The trail continues several miles farther, however, you eventually have to turn around and come out the same you way you entered. You can easily spend 2 to 4 hours exploring the area.

To Get There: Take Interstate 70 to Grand Junction. From the east side, take Exit 37 following Business 70 west to Route 340. Turn left on 340 and cross the Broadway Bridge. After the bridge, turn left on Monument Road. Go 0.1 miles and turn left again on "D" Road. After 0.3 miles, turn right and head south on Rosevale Road 0.9 miles to Little Park Road. Turn right and drive 5.0 miles to Bangs Canyon on the left.

From the west side, take Interstate 70 Exit 26 following US 6 east along the Colorado River until it reaches Route 340. Turn right and cross the Broadway Bridge. Turn left on Monument Road and follow the same directions as described above.

A third option is to take Interstate 70 Exit 31. Follow Horizon Drive southwest to 12th Street. Go south to Grand Avenue and turn right. Grand Avenue changes to Broadway before it reaches the Broadway Bridge. Follow the above directions after crossing the bridge.

Trail Description: *Reset your odometer as you turn off Little Park Road.* A prominent sign marks the Bangs Canyon Staging Area. Follow a gravel road 0.2 miles south to a parking area where the trail departs to the right. Bear left at 0.3 miles after crossing a cattle guard. At 0.7 miles, you encounter a large slab of rock. Bear left and follow the rock downhill. The trail is not well defined but if you continue downhill, you will eventually reach the bottom of the canyon. The right side of the trail is defined by the walls of the canyon. If you get too far to the right, the trail may dead-end where a finger projects into the canyon. If this happens, turn around and try a different route. Half the fun of this trail is exploring the area. The scenery is spectacular and the terrain offers all kinds of interesting driving options. Another trail comes in from the left at about 1.4 miles. You should reach the bottom of the canyon at about 2.2 miles if you take the most direct route to the bottom.

The bottom of the canyon is normally a dry creek bed but use caution if there are storms in the area. High water could block your path after a heavy rain. As you start up the other side, the road becomes more defined and gets increasingly difficult. A fairly tough spot is reached at 3.0 miles (see bottom photo on page 148). At 3.6 miles, the soil changes to bentonite clay which is a pale gray/green color. It is very slippery when wet, so use extreme caution under these conditions. The road winds up the mountainside and is fairly narrow in places. You'll cross a short section of private property at 4.6 miles. At 4.7 miles, a difficult spur road departs to the left. This road follows West Bangs Canyon for quite a few miles before it dead ends. You may continue about 4 more miles on the main trail before it turns to the northeast. From this point, the trail becomes less interesting and eventually dead-ends at private property after a considerable distance.

Return Trip: Return the way you came.

Services: Full services in Grand Junction.

Other Activities: This area is extremely popular for hiking and mountain biking. The well known Tabeguache Biking Trail follows much of the route described here and continues all the way to Montrose. Signs mark the trail along the way. During the summer, temperatures often climb above 100 degrees, so make sure you carry plenty of water and are properly dressed.

Maps: BLM Grand Junction Resource Area Map, Colorado Atlas and Gazetteer.

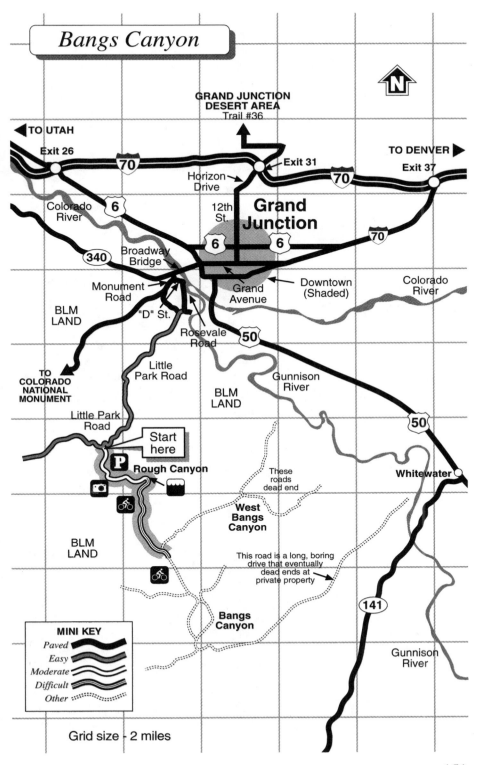

Bangs Canyon

N

GRAND JUNCTION DESERT AREA
Trail #36

◄ TO UTAH

Exit 26

70

TO DENVER ►

Exit 31

Exit 37

Horizon Drive

70

Colorado River

6

12th St.

Grand Junction

70

340

Broadway Bridge

6   **6**

Monument Road

"D" St.

Grand Avenue

Downtown (Shaded)

Colorado River

BLM LAND

Rosevale Road

50

TO COLORADO NATIONAL MONUMENT

Little Park Road

BLM LAND

Gunnison River

50

Little Park Road

Start here

P **Rough Canyon**

These roads dead end

Whitewater

West Bangs Canyon

BLM LAND

This road is a long, boring drive that eventually dead ends at private property

141

Bangs Canyon

Gunnison River

MINI KEY
Paved
Easy
Moderate
Difficult
Other

Grid size - 2 miles

151

One of several muddy water crossings.   Bonham Reservoir.

Long wheel-based vehicles will find narrow sections like this very difficult to get through.

This driver chose an aggressive route and got stuck.

Long Slough Res. Road ◆39◆

Location: East of Grand Junction. Southwest of Parachute.

Difficulty: Difficult. The middle portion of this trail is strictly hard-core and not suitable for stock sport utility vehicles. Challenges include mud bogs, tight brush, and narrow passages between trees. Full-size vehicles are not recommended. Parts of the trail are used primarily by motorcycles and ATVs, but the trail is open to aggressive four-wheelers. The first and last portions of the trail range from easy to moderate with occasional difficult sections.

Features: This road services an extensive network of reservoirs whose primary function is water collection and secondary function is recreational use. At certain times of the year, some of the reservoirs are drained. Although the trail is relatively flat, it is at a high elevation around 10,000 ft. Prepare for cooler temperatures and more frequent precipitation. There are beautiful views getting to and from the trail, but the trail itself is not scenic.

Time & Distance: The trail is about 13 miles long but five miles must be driven at a snail's pace. Allow 4 to 5 hours on the trail. It is also a long drive to and from the trail, so allow a full day for this trip.

To Get There: From Interstate 70 Exit 49, take Highway 65 east following signs to the Powderhorn Ski Area. About 5 miles past the ski area, turn left on F.S. 254 across from the F.S. Jumbo Lakes Campground.

Trail Description: Reset your odometer as you turn off Highway 65. After 0.3 miles turn right onto 254.1A. Bear left at 0.5 and right at 1.9 before reaching Long Slough Reservoir at 2.5 miles. Muddy spots become more frequent after going straight at 3.1 miles. At 4.3, go right, followed by two successive left turns at 4.5 miles. A mixture of mud and logs presents a challenge at 5.1 miles.

At 5.2, bear left before reaching a spillway for Bull Creek Reservoir No.5. After this point, the trail gets narrower and more difficult. Do not proceed unless you are prepared for a real challenge. At 5.5 miles, bear left at a cabin and left again at 6.6 miles. At 8.0 miles, turn right at a faint four-way intersection in the middle of a large meadow. More challenges remain before reaching a bog at 10.4 miles. You can get around the bog on the right but it is off-camber.

After passing the Currier Reservoir, turn left at 11.2 miles. At 11.9

153

miles, F.S. 259 enters from the left. You bear right, passing through a fence. You'll bear left at 12.1 before going by a water collection station. You reach the end of the trail at 12.8 miles where it intersects with Cottonwood Lakes Road F.S. 257.

Return Trip: Turn left on Cottonwood Lakes Road. Bear right when it intersects with F.S. 258 in about 1 mile. Continue another 3 miles. Pass the Bonham Reservoir, a Forest Service campground, and intersect with Trickle Park Road F.S. 121. There is a pit toilet at the campground. A right turn on Trickle Park Road will take you on a long drive back to Hwy. 65. If you turn left, Trickle Park Road soon becomes paved and eventually connects to County Rd. 330 near Collbran. Head west on 330 back to 65 at a point just north of the town of Mesa.

For Grand Junction, take 65 back to Interstate 70. For points east, take the De Beque Cut-Off Road north to Interstate 70.

You may also extend your backcountry trip by driving Kenney Creek Reservoir Road (Trail #40) in the opposite direction as described. To find the trail, drive 1.0 miles north on Trickle Park Road and turn right on F.S. 260.

Services: Full services in Grand Junction and Parachute. Gas and food is available in Collbran and Mesa. Pit toilets are available at the F.S. Jumbo Lakes Campground at the start of the trail and the Bonham Reservoir Campground at the end of the trip.

Other Activities: Fishing is a dominant activity in the area. Two Forest Service Campgrounds are located near the start of the trail on Hwy. 65. The Jumbo Lakes Campground is located across from the start of the trail and the Spruce Grove Campground is just a mile south on Hwy. 65. Picnicking and camping are also available at the Bonham Reservoir. Fishing, boating, and camping are available at Cottonwood Lake No. 1, which is just south of where the end of the trail joins Cottonwood Lakes Road. Snowmobiling and cross-country skiing are popular wintertime activities. Wear bright colors in the fall because this is a popular hunting area.

For more information about the area, stop in at the Grand Mesa Visitor Center. It is located about 10 miles south on Hwy. 65 past the start of the trail.

Maps: Grand Mesa National Forest, Trails Illustrated Grand Mesa #136, Colorado Atlas and Gazetteer.

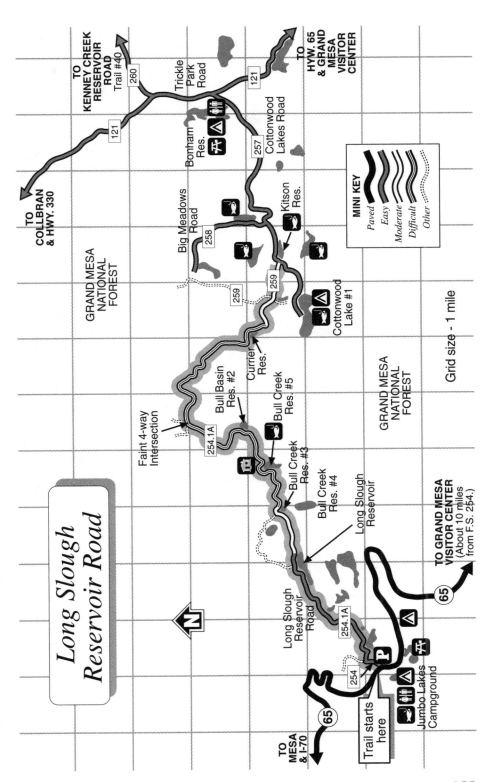

Long Slough Reservoir Road

MINI KEY
Paved
Easy
Moderate
Difficult
Other

Grid size - 1 mile

N

GRAND MESA NATIONAL FOREST

GRAND MESA NATIONAL FOREST

TO COLLBRAN & HWY. 330

TO KENNEY CREEK RESERVOIR ROAD Trail #40

260

121

121

Trickle Park Road

Bonham Res.

258

Big Meadows Road

257

Cottonwood Lakes Road

121

TO HWY. 65 & GRAND MESA VISITOR CENTER

Kitson Res.

259

259

Cottonwood Lake #1

Currier Res.

Bull Basin Res. #2

Faint 4-way Intersection

254.1A

Bull Creek Res. #5

Bull Creek Res. #3

Bull Creek Res. #4

Long Slough Reservoir

Long Slough Reservoir Road

254.1A

254

P

TO MESA & I-70

65

Trail starts here

Jumbo Lakes Campground

65

TO GRAND MESA VISITOR CENTER (About 10 miles from F.S. 254.)

155

Crossing Leon Creek from west to east. This photo was taken in the fall when water was low.

Looking down from above Kenney Creek Reservoir.

This creek crossing is a little narrow.

One of the rockiest sections of the trail.

Kenney Creek Res. Road 40

Location: West of Grand Junction. South of the Vega State Recreation Area.

Difficulty: Moderate. Much of this trail is easy but there are a few narrow rocky spots that offer moderate challenges. A stream crossing at the beginning of the trail can be deep in the spring. The trail is also muddy at times. It is best to wait until later in the summer if you are driving a stock sport utility vehicle. High ground clearance is recommended.

Features: The first part of this trail is an interesting and scenic drive. The last half has been graded. Interest can be added to the trip by exploring several spur roads. These roads have not been rated, so explore at your own risk. This trail is convenient to the popular Vega State Recreation Area.

Time & Distance: The trail, as shown here, is about 7.4 miles one way and takes about 2 hours. It's a long way to and from the trail, so allow adequate traveling time. If you are staying at the Vega State Recreation Area, you may wish to drive just the more interesting first half of the trail.

To Get There: From Grand Junction, head north on Interstate 70 to Exit 49. Then head east on Hwy. 65 to Hwy. 330. Continue east to Collbran and follow signs to the Vega State Recreation Area. There is a fee to enter the park, but you may not have to pay if you are just passing through. Ask the guard. After crossing the dam, turn right on Park Creek Road, F.S. 262, a wide gravel road. Drive about 7 miles south and watch for F.S. 260 on the right.

From points east, get off Interstate 70 at De Beque, Exit 62. Head south on the De Beque Cut-Off Road to Hwy. 65. Turn left for Hwy. 330. Head east to Collbran and follow same directions as above.

You can also run this trail in the reverse direction after completing Long Slough Reservoir Road (Trail #39). From Bonham Reservoir, head north on Trickle Park Road F.S. 121 about a mile and turn right on F.S. 260.

Trail Description: *Reset your odometer at the start.* Head west on F.S. 260. You immediately encounter Leon Creek. It's usually easy to cross but may be deeper in the spring. The road begins to climb and reaches a smaller stream crossing at 0.7 miles. You'll pass through some tight rocky sections before making a right turn at 0.9 miles. By 1.7 miles, you climb above Kenney Creek Reservoir where there are some nice photo opportunities. Bear right at 2.1 miles. At 3.4 miles, watch for a beautiful view of the mountains to the east. At 3.5 miles, the road widens before passing through a fence and over a cattle guard. The road is well maintained from this point with just an occasional muddy spot. Be careful—it's still possible to get stuck. Bear left at 3.8, right at 4.2, left at 5.2, right at 5.9, and left at 6.7. At 7.4 miles, you intersect a better quality road still marked as F.S. 260. Turn left and go about one mile to reach Trickle Park Road F.S. 121.

Return Trip: At Trickle Park Road, head north. The road becomes paved and eventually runs into Hwy. 330 at several places near Collbran. Head west on 330 to Hwy. 65. Turn right for Interstate 70. If you are heading to points east, take the De Beque Cut-Off Road north, as it departs from Hwy. 65 just a little north of Hwy. 330.

Services: Full services in Grand Junction and Parachute. Gas and food is available in Collbran and Mesa. Toilets are available at the Vega State Recreation Area and the Bonham Reservoir.

Other Activities: There are many Forest Service campgrounds and picnic areas at the Vega State Recreation Area in addition to boating and fishing. There is also a nice campground and picnic area at the Bonham Reservoir. Wear bright colors in the fall because this is a popular hunting area. In the winter, snowmobiling is the primary activity.

Maps: Grand Mesa National Forest, Trails Illustrated Grand Mesa #136, Colorado Atlas and Gazetteer.

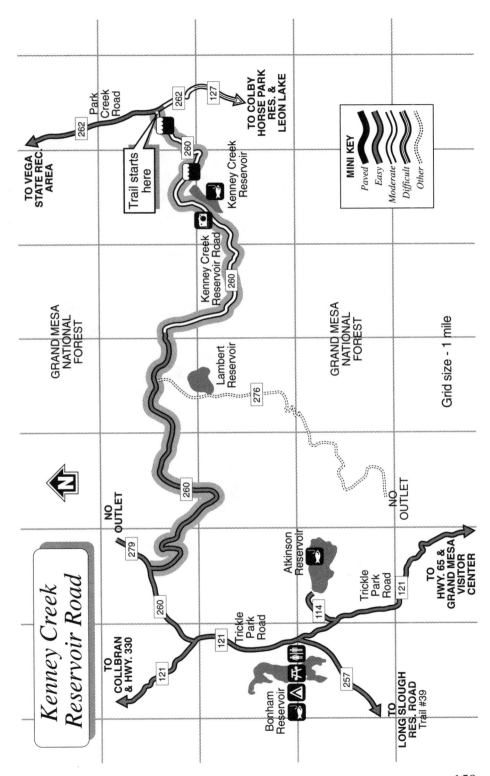

159

Crossing a ditch in the Grand Junction Desert, Trail #36, rated difficult.

APPENDIX

You pass through Colorado National Monument to reach Rattlesnake Canyon, Trail #37.

Glossary

Airing down - Letting air out of your tires to improve traction.

ARB lockers - A brand of differential locker that can be quickly activated when needed but turned off when not in use. (See differential locker.)

Articulation - The flexibility of your suspension system. Greater articulation means your wheels will go up and down more to better accommodate ground undulation.

BLM - Bureau of Land Management.

Boulder fields - Challenging stretches of rocky terrain.

C.G. - Campground.

Clevis - A U-shaped device with a pin at one end that is used to connect tow straps.

Come-along - A hand-operated ratchet that functions as a winch.

Crossbuck fence- A free-standing log fence supported by X braces instead of fence posts. (See upper right photo on page 68.)

Differential locker - Optional gearing installed inside your differential that equalizes power to wheels on both sides of an axle. Eliminates loss of power when climbing steep undulating hills. Not the same as locking-in your hubs.

F.S. - Forest Service.

Hard-core - The most challenging level of four-wheeling.

High centered - When your undercarriage gets stuck on a rock, mound, log, or ridge. Usually requires you to jack up your vehicle to get free.

High lift jack - A tool that allows you to quickly lift your vehicle high off the ground. Considered a necessity on hard-core trails. Also substitutes for a winch.

Lift - A vehicle modification that raises the suspension or body of a vehicle to provide greater ground clearance.

Locker - (See differential locker.)

Low range - A second range of gears that increases the power of your vehicle. Used for climbing steep grades, especially at higher altitude.

Marmot - A bushy-tailed, stocky rodent native to high mountain terrain. Makes a distinctive high-pitch chirping sound. Nicknamed " Whistle Pigs."

Moguls - Large bumps which form on steep hills.

Off-camber - The sideways lean of a vehicle away from a slope.

Shelf road - A narrow road cut into a mountainside.

Skid plates - Plates that protect vulnerable parts of your undercarriage.

Snatch block - A pulley that opens so it can be slipped over your winch cable.

Spur road - A side road that is usually narrower and rougher than the main road.

SUV - Sport Utility Vehicle.

Switchback - A zig-zag road for climbing a steep grade.

Talus -Loose fragmented rock formed by freezing and thawing above timberline.

Timberline - The point on a mountainside where trees stop growing. In Colorado about 11,000 ft.

Tow point, tow hook - A point on your vehicle that enables you to quickly and safely attach a tow strap. Considered a basic necessity for four-wheeling.

Tow strap - A heavy-duty nylon strap used to pull vehicles when stuck.

Tree strap - A short tow strap that is used to wrap around trees and large rocks.

References & Reading

(The) Big Thompson Flood, by Don Cotten, C.F. Boone, Publisher, Lubbock, TX. A compilation of newspaper stories, original stories, and photographs printed shortly after the disaster. (1976)

Colorado: A Bicentennial History, by Marshall Sprague, W. W. Norton & Company, Inc., New York, N.Y.. A formal textbook on the general history of Colorado primarily covering the last 200 years. (1976)

Colorado Ghost Towns Past and Present, by Robert L. Brown, Caxton Printers, Ltd., Caldwell, ID. Historical descriptions of Colorado ghost towns. Photos compare yesteryear to present. (First printing 1972, revised several times)

A Colorado History, by Carl Ubbelohde, Maxine Benson, Duane A. Smith, Pruett Publishing, Boulder, CO. A formal textbook on the general history of Colorado covering A.D. 1 to 1982. (1982)

(The) Colorado Pass Book, by Don Koch, Pruett Publishing Company, Boulder, CO. Illustrated guide to Colorado passroads with in-depth historical analysis. Large, quality photographs. (Revised 1992)

Ghost Towns of the Colorado Rockies, by Robert L. Brown, Caxton Printers, Ltd., Caldwell, ID. Historical descriptions of Colorado ghost towns. Photos compare yesteryear to present. (First printing 1968, revised several times)

Jeep Trails to Colorado Ghost Towns, by Robert L. Brown, Caxton Printers, Ltd., Caldwell, ID. Historical descriptions of Colorado ghost towns. Photos compare yesteryear to present. (First printing 1963, revised several times)

(The) Moffat Road, Published by the Rollins Pass Restoration Association, Longmont, CO. A twenty-page self-guided auto tour of Rollins Pass. Includes brief history and points of interest along the route. (1996)

(The) Roads of Colorado, Shearer Publishing, Fredericksburg, TX. A complete atlas of Colorado dividing the state into 144 rectangular sections. Includes main roads and most backroads of Colorado, historical glimpses, and many other facts about Colorado. (1996)

Scenic Driving Colorado, by Stewart Green, Falcon Press Publishing Co., Inc., Helena & Billings, MT. Scenic drives for passenger cars with maps and photos. (1994)

Tread Lightly! Guide to Responsible Four-Wheeling, Published by *Tread Lightly!*, Inc. Ogden, UT. Illustrated guide featuring minimum impact four-wheel drive techniques and safety tips. (1997)

4 x 4 Trail Books, by the Colorado Association of 4 Wheel Drive Clubs, Inc. Wheatridge, CO. A series of four guidebooks with maps and descriptions covering primarily hard-core trails of Colorado. (1989-1996)

Addresses & Phone Numbers

Bureau of Land Management Offices (Selected Locations):

COLORADO STATE OFFICE
2850 Youngfield Street
Lakewood, CO 80215
(303) 239- 3600

CRAIG DISTRICT OFFICE
455 Emerson Street
Craig, CO 81625
(970) 826-5000

Kremmling Resource Area
1116 Park Ave.
P.O. Box 68
Kremmling, CO 80459
(970) 724-3437

GRAND JUNCTION DISTRICT OFFICE and Resource Area
2815 H Road
Grand Junction, CO 81506
(970) 244-3000

MONTROSE DISTRICT OFFICE
2465 South Townsend
Montrose, CO 81401
(970) 249-7791

Chambers of Commerce numbers for cities near the trails:

Boulder	(303) 442-1044
Broomfield	(303) 466-1775
Central City	(303) 582-5077
Craig	(970) 824-5689
Denver:	
Greater Denver	(303) 534-8500
Metro North	(303) 450-0335
Northwest Metro	(303) 424-0313
South Metro	(303) 795-0142
West	(303) 233-5555
Estes Park	(970) 586-4431
Evergreen	(800) 472-8230
Fort Collins	(970) 482-3746
Fruita	(970) 858-3894
Georgetown	(303) 569-2888
Gilpin County	(303) 582-5077
Golden	(303) 279-3113
Granby	(970) 887-2311
Grand Junction	(970) 242-3214
Grand Lake	(970) 627-3372
Greeley/Weld	(970) 352-3566
Kremmling	(970) 724-3472
Longmont	(303) 776-5295
Loveland	(970) 667-6311
Lyons	(303) 823-5215
Nederland	(303) 258-3936
North Park	(970) 723-4600
Steamboat Springs	(970) 879-0880
Winter Park	(970) 726-4118

Four Wheel Drive Organizations & Support Groups:

BLUERIBBON COALITION
1540 North Arthur Ave.
Pocatello, ID 83204
(208) 233-6570

COLORADO ASSOCIATION OF 4-WHEEL DRIVE CLUBS, INC.
P.O. Box 1413
Wheat Ridge, CO 80034
(303) 343-0646

ROLLINS PASS RESTORATION ASSOCIATION
P.O. Box 1082
Longmont, CO 80502-1082

TREAD LIGHTLY, INC.
298 24th Street
Suite 325
Ogden, UT 84401
(800) 966-9900

UNITED FOUR WHEEL DRIVE ASSOCIATIONS, INC.
4505 W. 700 S.
Shelbyville, IN 46176-9678
1 (800) 448-3932

National Forest Service & Ranger Districts (Selected Locations):

ARAPAHO/ROOSEVELT NATIONAL FORESTS
240 West Prospect Road
Fort Collins, CO 80526
(970) 498-1100

Boulder Ranger District
2995 Baseline Road
Room 110
Boulder, CO 80303
(303) 444-6600

Clear Creek Ranger District
101 Chicago Creek
Idaho Springs, CO 80452
(303) 567-2901

Canyon Lakes Ranger District
(Formerly Estes/Poudre and
 Red Feather Ranger Districts)
1311 South College
Fort Collins, CO 80524
(970) 498-1367

Sulphur Ranger District
9 Ten Mile Drive
Granby, CO 80446
(970) 887-4100

ROUTT NATIONAL FOREST
925 Weiss Drive
Steamboat Springs, CO 80487-9315
(970) 879-1870

Hahns Peak/Bear Ears Ranger District
925 Weiss Drive
Steamboat Springs, CO
80487-9315
(970) 879-1870

Parks Ranger District
100 Main Street
P.O. Box 158
Walden, CO 80480
(970) 723-8204

UNCOMPAHGRE NATIONAL FOREST
2505 South Townsend
Montrose, CO 81401
(970) 240-5300

Grand Junction Ranger District
2777 Crossroads Blvd.-Unit A
Grand Junction, CO 81506
(970) 242-8211

WHITE RIVER NATIONAL FOREST
9th and Grand
P.O. Box 948
Glenwood Springs, CO 81601
(970) 945-2521

National/State Parks and Monuments:

COLORADO NATIONAL MONUMENT
Fruita, CO 81521
(970) 858-3617

COLORADO STATE PARKS
1313 Sherman Street
Room 618
Denver, CO 80203
(303) 866-3437

GOLDEN GATE CANYON STATE PARK
3873 Hwy. 46
Golden, CO 80403
(303) 582-3707

ROCKY MOUNTAIN NATIONAL PARK
Estes Park, CO 80517
(970) 586-1206

Other Information:

BLOWDOWN AREA HOTLINE
(970) 870-2192

CAMPING INFORMATION HOTLINE
1-800-678-2267

COLORADO STATE FOREST/ STATE PARK
2746 Jackson City Road 41
Walden, CO 80480
(970) 723-8366

N.F. CAMPING RESERVATIONS
1-800-280-2267

Index

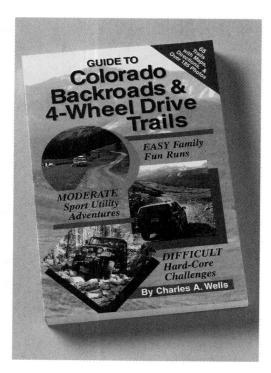

Praise for the original guide:

"Neither a stranger to Colorado nor an experienced resident will go wrong with this important guide to our most mountainous state, especially given its modest cover price. Don't shift into 4-wheel drive without it."
Spencer Murray,
Open Road Magazine

"A concise guide to Colorado's remote back-country"...
Today's Sport Utility Vehicle Magazine

"Fourwheelin' in Colorado is explained fully in this great new guide...(it) gives details of 65 routes including 47 for stock SUVs"....
John Carroll, *Land Rover World Magazine*

"This guide is worth its weight in accuracy and information, and would be perfect for any families or individuals looking for backcountry adventures in scenic Colorado."
Jennifer Swatsenbarg, *BlueRibbon Magazine*

"Long-awaited and highly sought by avid four-wheeling clients, Chuck Wells has created our first Colorado four-wheel-drive guide and we think it's incredibly comprehensive. It's a winner on all counts, and about time!"
John Stone, *The Chinook Bookshop, Inc.*

"Our best selling book in 1998."
Dave Rich, *Books West*
Colorado's largest in-state book distributor

"Wells' book is perfect for 4-wheel-drive fans and wannabes, and could even help hikers plan trips that use 4-wheel-drive roads as their beginnings or ends."
Deb Acord, *The Colorado Springs Gazette*

Trail listing for the *original* guide:

The original *Guide to Colorado Backroads & 4-Wheel Drive Trails* is the same convenient 6" x 9" size and contains 248 pages. It covers 65 popular trails in Colorado. The format and quality of the book are exactly the same as Volume 2. Below is a listing of all 65 trails grouped into seven areas. Nineteen trails are rated easy (E), 28 moderate (M), and 18 difficult (D). Forty-seven are suitable for most stock sport utility vehicles. To order, see the order blanks in the back of this book or turn to page 2.

Area 1
Ouray, Silverton, Lake City, Telluride
1. Owl Creek Pass (E)
2. Yankee Boy Basin (M)
3. Imogene Pass (M)
4. Black Bear Pass (D)
5. Ophir Pass (M)
6. Clear Lake (M)
7. Engineer Pass (M)
8. Cinnamon Pass (M)
9. Poughkeepsie Gulch (D)
10. Picayne & Placer Gulch (M)
11. Corkscrew Gulch (M)
12. California Gulch (M)
13. Eureka Gulch (E)
14. Nellie Creek (M)
15. Stony Pass (M)
16. Maggie Gulch (E)
17. Minnie Gulch (M)
18. Wager Gulch (M)

Area 2
Crested Butte, Aspen, Marble
19. Schofield Pass, Crystal River (D)
20. Lead King Basin (D)
21. Kebler & Ohio Pass (E)
22. Gunsight Pass (M)
23. Slate & Gothic Road (E)
24. Pearl Pass (D)
25. Taylor Pass (D)
26. Italian Creek Road (D)

Area 3
Buena Vista, Monarch
27. Tincup Pass (M)
28. Mt. Princeton (M)
29. Sevenmile Road (E)
30. Waunita & Black Sage Pass (E)
31. Tomichi Pass (D)
32. Hancock Pass, Alpine Tunnel (M)
33. Mt. Antero (D)
34. Cumberland Pass (E)

35. Old Monarch Pass (E)
36. Pomeroy Lake Road (M)
37. Iron Chest (D)

Area 4
Vail, Leadville, Fairplay
38. West Lake Creek Road (E)
39. Shrine Pass (E)
40. Holy Cross (D)
41. McCallister Gulch (M)
42. Ptarmigan Pass (M)
43. Wheeler Lake (D)
44. Hagerman Pass (M)
45. Mt. Lincoln (M)
46. Mosquito Pass (M)
47. Mt. Bross (M)
48. Weston Pass (E)

Area 5
Breckenridge, Dillon, Como, Idaho Springs
49. Boreas Pass (E)
50. Georgia Pass (M)
51. Webster Pass (D)
52. Red Cone (D)
53. Lamartine, Saxton Road (E)
54. Spring Creek (D)
55. Guanella Pass (E)

Area 6
Pikes Peak Region
56. La Salle Pass (E)
57. Mt. Herman Road (E)
58. Longwater Gulch (D)
59. Hackett Gulch (D)
60. Rampart Range Road (E)
61. Mt. Baldy (M)
62. Phantom Canyon, Shelf Road (E)

Area 7
Sangre De Cristo Mountain Range
63. Hayden Pass (M)
64. Medano Pass (M)
65. Blanca Peak (D)

About the Author

Charles A. Wells graduated from Ohio State University in 1969 with a degree in graphic design. After practicing design in Ohio, he moved to Colorado Springs in 1980 and worked 18 years in the printing business. He and his wife, Beverly, raised two children who have graduated from Colorado universities. Over the years, he and his family have enjoyed a wide array of recreational activities including hiking, biking, rafting, and skiing. This exposure to the Colorado backcountry led to his interest in four-wheeling in recent years. He became frustrated when he could not find a clear, simple backroad guide to Colorado; so he decided to write his own.

All of the trails in this book were driven by the author in the vehicles described below. He wrote the trail descriptions based on his own observations, shot all the photographs, and created all the maps. No sponsors were involved. The result of this hands-on approach is a valuable and unbiased reference for both novices and hard-core four-wheeling enthusiasts.

Author with Jeep Grand Cherokee on Storm Mountain. Equipped with automatic transmission, factory skid plates, tow points, all-terrain tires, and CB radio.

Jeep is a registered trademark of Chrysler Corporation.

Jeep Cherokee on Yankee Hill Road. Equipped with Tomken 5 1/2" lift, bumpers, rocker skids, tire carrier, and brush guard; 8,000 lb. Warn winch mounts front & rear; Dana 44 rear axle; 410 gears; ARBs front & rear; skid plates; stock 4-liter engine with 5-speed; K&N air filter; full interior roll cage; 32 x 11.50 BFG A/T tires; Optima battery; tow points; fold-in mirrors; and CB radio.

Order Form

 Phone orders: Call toll free 1-(877) 222-7623. We accept VISA and MasterCard.

 Postal orders: Send check, name, address, and telephone number to: FunTreks, Inc. P.O. Box 49187, Colorado Springs, CO 80949-9187. If paying by credit card, include your VISA or MasterCard number and expiration date.

 Fax orders: Fax this order form to 1-(719) 277-7411. Include your VISA or MasterCard number and expiration date.

Please send me the following book(s):

I understand that if I am not completely satisfied, I may return the book(s) for a full refund, no questions asked.

Qty.

❏ *Guide to Colorado Backroads & 4-Wheel Drive Trails, (Original)* _____
      ISBN 0-9664976-0-0, 248 pages, Price $18.95

❏ *Guide to Colorado Backroads & 4-Wheel Drive Trails Vol. 2* _____
      ISBN 0-9664976-1-9, 176 pages, Price $15.95

❏ Other _____ _____

Billing address:
Name: _____
Address: _____
City: _____State: _____Zip: _____
Telephone: (____) _____

Shipping address: (Not necessary if same as above)
Name: _____
Address: _____
City: _____State: _____Zip: _____
Telephone: (____) _____

Sales Tax: Please add 3% for books shipped to Colorado.

Shipping: $4.00 for the first book and $2.00 for each additional book.

Payment: ❏ Check   ❏ VISA   ❏ MasterCard
Card number:_____Exp. date:_____
Name on card:_____

Call toll free 1-(877) 222-7623 -Thanks for your order

Order Form

 Phone orders: Call toll free 1-(877) 222-7623. We accept VISA and MasterCard.

 Postal orders: Send check, name, address, and telephone number to: FunTreks, Inc. P.O. Box 49187, Colorado Springs, CO 80949-9187. If paying by credit card, include your VISA or MasterCard number and expiration date.

 Fax orders: Fax this order form to 1-(719) 277-7411. Include your VISA or MasterCard number and expiration date.

Please send me the following book(s):

I understand that if I am not completely satisfied, I may return the book(s) for a full refund, no questions asked.

Qty.

❏ *Guide to Colorado Backroads & 4-Wheel Drive Trails, (Original)* _____
ISBN 0-9664976-0-0, 248 pages, Price $18.95

❏ *Guide to Colorado Backroads & 4-Wheel Drive Trails Vol. 2* _____
ISBN 0-9664976-1-9, 176 pages, Price $15.95

❏ Other _____ _____

Billing address:
Name: _____
Address: _____
City: _____State: _____Zip: _____
Telephone: (_____) _____

Shipping address: (Not necessary if same as above)
Name: _____
Address: _____
City: _____State: _____Zip: _____
Telephone: (_____) _____

Sales Tax: Please add 3% for books shipped to Colorado.

Shipping: $4.00 for the first book and $2.00 for each additional book.

Payment: ❏ Check   ❏ VISA   ❏ MasterCard
Card number:_____Exp. date:_____
Name on card:_____

Call toll free 1-(877) 222-7623 -Thanks for your order